GUIDED SELF-HEALING MEDITATIONS

Chakras for Beginners, Deep Sleep Techniques, Anxiety, Stress, Depression therapy, Panic Attacks, Breathing, insomnia, Awakening Secrets, and Mindfulness

© Spiritual Awakening Academy

GUIDED SELF-HEALING MEDITATION

Table of Contents

INTRODUCTION   5

CHAPTER ONE: HISTORY OF MEDITATION   5
- THE BASICS OF MEDITATION   12
- BENEFITS OF MEDITATION   15
  - *Meditation Helps to Reduce Stress*   15
  - *Meditation Helps Keep Emotions under Control*   16
  - *Meditation Increases Serotonin Secretion*   17
  - *Meditation Improves the Ability to Focus*   17
  - *Meditation Increases Creativity*   18
  - *Meditation Increases Empathy and the Ability to Connect*   18
  - *Meditation Helps Improve Relationships*   19
  - *Meditation Enhances Memory*   19
  - *Meditation Improves Immunity*   20
  - *Meditation Helps You Overcome Addictions*   20
  - *Meditation Benefits Cardiovascular Health*   21
  - *Meditation Aids Weight Loss*   23
  - *Meditation Helps Manage Headaches*   24
- HOW TO ESTABLISH A GOOD MEDITATION PRACTICE?   26
  - *It helps you create a habit*   27
- CHAKRA HEALING MEDITATION   30

CHAPTER TWO: ANXIETY   40
- *Strained Communication*   41
- *Toxic Personality*   41
- *Former Relationship*   42
- *Gratefulness*   42
- *Work-Related Stress*   43
- *It Keeps You Positive*   43
- *Your Connection*   44
- THE FIVE TYPES OF ANXIETY DISORDERS   45
  - *Social Phobias (Social Anxiety Disorder)*   45
  - *Generalized Anxiety Disorder (GAD)*   46
  - *Post-Traumatic Stress Disorder (PTSD)*   46
  - *Panic Disorder*   47

Obsessive-Compulsive Disorder (OCD)	47
EASY STEPS TO HELP YOU OVERCOME ANXIETY IN YOUR RELATIONSHIP	48
Difficulties in This Meditation	52
How to Practice Meditation for GAD	54

CHAPTER THREE: HOW TO CALM THE BODY 56

Mindfulness Body Scan Meditation	61
Breathing Exercises throughout the Day	64

CHAPTER FOUR: HOW TO CALM THE MIND 77

Why You Should Calm Your Mind	78
How to Calm Your Mind through Meditation	83
Through Mindfulness	88

CHAPTER FIVE: GUIDED MEDITATION TO MANAGE PANIC ATTACK 97

SYMPTOMS OF PANIC ATTACKS:	97
THUNDEROUS HEARTBEAT	97
FEELING OF WEAKNESS	98
NUMBNESS IN THE FINGERS AND TOES	98
AN IMPENDING SENSE OF DOOM	99
SWEATING	99
CHEST PAINS	99
DIFFICULTY IN BREATHING	99
NO CONTROL	100
DEREALIZATION	100
TIPS FOR DEALING WITH PANIC ATTACKS	100
KNOWLEDGE	101
BE CALM	101
KNOW WHAT TRIGGERS YOUR PANIC ATTACKS	102
MINDFUL BREATHING	103
VISUALIZATION	104
BE COURAGEOUS	106
SURROUND YOURSELF WITH FRIENDS	107

CHAPTER SIX: DEEP SLEEP TECHNIQUES 115

MEDITATION TO OVERCOME INSOMNIA	115
MEDITATION TECHNIQUES FOR INSOMNIA	117

GUIDED SELF-HEALING MEDITATION

GUIDED MEDITATION TIPS FOR INSOMNIA	122
GUIDED MEDITATION FOR INSOMNIA IN PREGNANT WOMEN	128
GUIDED MEDITATION FOR INSOMNIA IN CHILDREN	132
CONCLUSION	**137**

Introduction
Chapter One: History Of Meditation

Meditation is slowly becoming a common practice in which many people see it differently. Perception is an individual's choice, and without knowledge and understanding, many would have different opinions about something. It is common for people to get to a place of familiarization with the practices and beliefs that they have previously believed to be meditation. An example is when people say meditation is a way of making the mind quiet; yet, that is not what meditation is about.

Several books have been written that relate to the meditation subject. Even so, confusion may arise because they have been written from the point of views dependent on standards and beliefs of a specific religions or philosophies. Some have made statements and values about meditation that sound like general laws, but generally meditation is a highly accurate procedure that is exclusive to a specific system of practice.

What Meditation Is Not?

GUIDED SELF-HEALING MEDITATION

There are several misconceptions about meditation which include:

- Meditation is just a relaxation technique – It should be well understood that meditation is not relaxation. A good example is when we sleep, sleeping and relaxing are not the same, but the critical connection is when we sleep, the result is relaxation. The same principle applies to meditation, one of the outcomes of meditation is relaxing when one sits straight for a specific period of time and relax that does not end the duality nature of the mind. It is essential to understand that relaxing is one of the beneficial results of meditation. It relaxes you, rejuvenates and makes one calm giving a sense of serenity.

- Meditation is meant for people on a spiritual search – Contrary to the misconception, meditation is for anybody wishing to tap into its manifold of benefits. One of the primary purposes is the ability to yield a relaxed mood making one aware of who they are without much effort. It is a vital tool for everyone because anyone and everyone would wish to know more about themselves without having to depend on someone else to tell them, and this is only achievable through meditation.

- Meditation is not concentration or contemplation – When one focuses on something or concentrates, they are merely narrowing the awareness. One can only focus on one specific object after the exclusion of everything else. Meditation is all-inclusive as your consciousness is expanded. When one meditates, they become aware but not of anything specific or particular. Meditation is simply one of the forms of concentration. Concentration makes one to always project their attention towards a specific task or activity while in meditation. The idea of projection of your attention to a particular job or business is not there. What meditation is capable of doing is giving one the ability to remain aware of the moment without selecting anything, in particular, to concentrate upon. Concentration is an art that helps one when learning meditation, especially at the initial stages, but it is not meditation.

- Meditation is not a religious practice – Perception has it that the sitting in a particular posture, chanting some specific, compelling words with a phonetic significance and the burning of essence is meditation. Meditation is neither the art of doing a particular exercise in a specific posture for a specific length of time. It is true that one has to take some time and give it some genuine effort and dedication for one to learn meditation, but that does not make it a religion or ritual. Meditation is simply the quality of one's existence which occurs when one gets to be aware of their true self and ae able to perform anything with awareness. Anyone, without focusing on religion, ethnicity, age, sex, creed or nationality can practice meditation. Once understood, meditation is more fun to do it does not involve any form of straining.

- Meditation is not a state of mind – We say meditation is not a state of mind, but it is the state of no-mind. We cannot say meditation is what one thinks; no, meditation is actually more than what one feels as it helps to find a peaceful place that is right inside you all the time. There are basically four states of mind according to scientists who are dependent on the frequency of mind waves. The four states are referred to as alpha, beta, gamma, and theta. When we say one is at the beta state, it merely means the state in which we live and perform all our day to day activities. The alpha is right below beta which is the state of meditation. Gamma and theta are the states of mind of further depth. At the alpha stage, it allows one to become still, tranquil and calm without any levels of stress or tension; in short, one becomes peaceful. Alpha is not meditation, but it is the state of mind in meditation. There is no gadget or mechanical device that can be used to create awareness, but the gadgets can only be used to create the right conditions which help us to realize what is true.

- Meditation is not self-hypnosis – As it is required in self-hypnosis, so it is the same in meditation because there is a need for an object of concentration in both cases. However, when meditating, the person who is involved has to maintain an awareness of here and now and equally stay very conscious and not to black out their mind. It is not a subconscious state that is usually the case with hypnosis. Hypnosis tries to turn one into an emotionless vegetable and makes the subject to be more susceptible to be controlled by another party. On the other hand, meditation makes one to become more and keener on their emotional changes. One gets to learn themselves with greater clarity and precision.

- Meditation is not a mysterious practice – Meditation is an art that deals with different levels of consciousness that lie more profound than the symbolic thought. The only interesting thing is that there may not be exact words to define meditation but that applies to different other things like we all understand how to walk but many of us, if not all, have the precise explanation of the order which the nerve fiber and muscles are able to contract during the whole process of our day to day everyday activity like walking. The same applies to meditation; we might not explain it in detail, but we can do it. When doing meditation, one cannot predict the outcome because it is merely an investigation or experiment and equally an adventure to look forward to.

- The purpose of meditation is to become a psychic – This is a misconception that people have that the end result of meditation is to be a psychic superman. The details like reading minds and levitation are not the ultimate goals in meditation, but the ultimate goal is self-liberation.

The Basics of Meditation

Meditation is what brings about personal change and addresses our own fundamental problems. When meditation is done with a focus on beliefs and theories instead of focusing on facts, then it seizes to be real. Taking a look at the daily happenings in life leaves us at a state where we realize many problems with lots of individual suffering, making several things in life to seem impossible and unachievable. With such unimaginable and unbearable pain, the only thing that helps us to see the world differently and focus on changing the world is meditation. Even for having our spirituality set right, it is vital to have the practical and realistic facts set right with a focus on dealing with the sufferings.

The following basic steps are necessary;

- As you start to train yourself on the art of meditation, it is crucial to try and sit at least every day even if it is just for five minutes; those five minutes will make a big difference. A key factor to consider is the regularity with which one practices the skill of meditation as it helps your memory to be aware of what is happening with you and your surroundings at any given time. The meditation done every day can be done invariance so that one engages in different activities for a varying length of time and a different skill on how to do it provided there is always something that one is doing daily. In any day things happen; differently, our day kickers keep changing, and that can make our emotions change taking us off the course, but the meditation practice is vital as it could be of great help to help us re-establish ourselves.

- The seat is not anything specific it can be a chai, a bench, the bed, a park bench or just some good-looking ground surface. The issue is getting somewhere comfortable, stable and solid so that at the end of the session you are not left feeling tired and fatigued remember our focus is on relaxing

- When meditating, you should equally be keen on the posture of the bottom half of the body. In case one is seated on a cushion, then you can cross your legs comfortably in front of you, making sure the knees are at the same level or below the hips. In case you are seated on a chair, then it is important that you have your feet on the floor with the foot fully touching the floor.

- Torso or upper part of the body should be straight without stiffening the spine. Let the spine have its natural curvature and create feeling that you are upright and very comfortable.

- The upper part of the arms is parallel with the torso while we let our hands drop and rest naturally; the idea of having identical sides helps to keep you from hunching over or being stiff.

- Focus on the head and eyes is that during meditation we drop the chin lower and allow a lower gaze which creates a humbling effect, then one can close their eyes and take time to relax because closing the eyes helps one to shift their concentration.

- Now it is time to pay attention to the mind and body interaction and the breath. Follow how you breathe out and in and be settled. Take a moment to consider yourself the best-dignified rider and enjoy a horse ride through life. You can make this a daily routine that will lead to self-awareness.

- Stay on course without letting your mind to wander, and if it does, it is advisable that you come back to your breath.

It is not possible to make ourselves any different just the same way we can't force a flower to grow. However, it is important that we establish some new conditions that can be of help in a gentle, skillful and gradual way to change our experiences. It is believed that our problems begin with the state of our minds, and we can fight the same problems which using the mind itself. It is risky when the mind sticks to the state of depression, anger or pain. Our emotions also cause our thoughts to interpret and view things from the perspective of how things are happening. As such, it is important to have a skilled meditator to take you through the guidelines and training on how to meditate in a manner that actively shape our minds. Therefore, we can say that real meditation is the form of perception that allows our consciousness to stay awake and free of conditioning. We all perceive or sense through the eyes, nose, ears, skin, and tongue but meditation is not done on the basis of these senses but on the perception with a different range of sense and power which is present in everyone.

Benefits of meditation

Meditation Helps to Reduce Stress

The modern-day lifestyle that we lead is hectic and inadvertently leads to stress and anxiety on some level. Stress has become one of the most common problems that people suffer from these days. You may think that you can put it off or might have resigned yourself to the fact that it is a part of your life. However, stress can lead to a myriad of health problems like high blood pressure, an increase in the risk of cardiovascular disorders, and insomnia, just to name a few. The stress chemical in the body is called cortisol. Your body can usually regulate the levels of cortisol within it, but the more your stress levels, the higher the amount of cortisol secreted. This can cause issues like panic attacks. Cortisol secretion needs to be regulated. All of these issues can, however, be dealt with using the help of meditation. It will help in reducing your stress levels and help you deal with anxiety-inducing issues in a productive manner. Overall, by practicing meditation, you will notice a decline in your stress and anxiety levels.

Meditation Helps Keep Emotions under Control

Humans are emotional creatures. However, it can be hard for us to control our emotions at times, and this can have dangerous consequences. This is especially true in the present world that we live in. The increased amount of pressure and anxiety you experience can cause a build-up of many negative feelings. If you let emotions like anger build-up, it will only harm you. Not just you, but also those around you. Meditation will help you maintain your calm and stay composed even in the face of adversity. When you are able to stay calm, then it is easier to rationalize your thoughts. Apart from this, it will also help you make better decisions. You must not let your emotions control you, and meditation will help you get a handle on your emotions.

Meditation Increases Serotonin Secretion

You might have heard of serotonin, the "happy hormone." The human body secretes various hormones that have a huge impact on how you think and feel. These chemicals in your body will affect how happy, sad, or angry you are. Serotonin is a chemical that helps people stay happy. Studies show that regular meditation helps in increasing serotonin secretion. This chemical has a positive effect on your mind and body. Low levels of serotonin are observed in people suffering from depression and other mental health issues. So, meditation is one of the most effective means of tackling depression.

Meditation Improves the Ability to Focus

Having the ability to focus better is something everyone aims for in life. However, most people have trouble with this. Being able to focus can help you in so many ways. If you are a student, it will help you study better. If you have specific goals in life, you will be able to focus on those goals and work accordingly. Lack of focus can make you lose track of what you do and lead an undisciplined life. Research shows that those who practice meditation tend to have a better ability to focus on their tasks and perform better than those who don't practice meditation. Different meditation techniques will help you hone your ability to focus and enhance your cognitive skills.

Meditation Increases Creativity

It is also said that meditation can get your creative juices flowing. When you meditate and reduce your stress levels, your brain is allowed to function better, and you can be more creative. This creative ability is often negatively impacted by high-stress levels. Meditation will help you embrace the good and the bad in your life without harming your happiness or health.

Meditation Increases Empathy and the Ability to Connect

You need to learn how to empathize and connect with others if you want better relationships. Meditation will help you learn compassion and thus act compassionately towards people. People who meditate tend to have an increased capacity for kindness and understanding towards others. You will be able to think of things from others' perspectives and react to situations in a better way. Meditation can enhance this empathetic ability and improve your social interactions.

Meditation Helps Improve Relationships

Do you feel like your relationships with your loved ones could use some extra help? Meditation can help you with this. Meditation helps increase your empathy, and this will help you immensely. It helps to increase your awareness so that you can pick up on cues from those around you. This will help you understand how they are feeling in certain situations. By getting a read on the situation, it will be easier for you to react and respond in the right way. Apart from this, it also helps reduce any chances of misunderstandings cropping up. Once your emotions are stabilized, the chances of letting any negativity through will decrease.

Meditation Enhances Memory

Do you feel like you have become forgetful? There could be many reasons behind this, stress being the main culprit. Regardless of what the cause is, meditation can help improve your memory, if practiced regularly. You will be able to focus on things and become more conscious of your surroundings and your own self. You will also be able to retain information for longer and thus be less forgetful. Meditation can be a great memory-enhancing tool regardless of what you do or what your age is.

Meditation Improves Immunity

Another benefit of meditation is that it is a holistic way of boosting your body's immune system. If you feel like you get sick too often or just want to be healthier, you should try meditation. Various meditation techniques like yoga are known to help in strengthening the immune system. By meditating regularly, you will notice a positive change in your overall immunity.

Meditation Helps You Overcome Addictions

Addictions are a serious affliction that can be really hard to contend with. It requires a lot of self-control and discipline to let go of any type of addiction. This could be smoking, alcoholism, or just about any unhealthy habit that has a negative impact on your health and well-being. It's not just the addictions that affect your physical health. There are other addictions like watching too much pornography, using excessive social media, binge eating, etc. These change your body and mind in many negative ways. There are certain meditation techniques, like Vipassana meditation, which is often used to help addicts overcome powerful addictions. Just meditating will not solve all your problems, but it is a great tool to help you move forward and leave your addictions behind. So, if you or anyone you know suffers from an addiction, trying meditation is a good place to start.

Meditation Benefits Cardiovascular Health

It is actually common sense that meditation is good for the heart. If you observe how regular meditation helps you when you need to relax and how it decreases your tendency to be anxious, at that point, is there any good reason why it shouldn't also help reduce the risk of cardiovascular issues, similar to hypertension?

For a considerable length of time, many assumed that to be the case, yet a couple of specialists appeared to be intrigued enough to research and document the physical outcomes on the heart after meditating. The leading researcher to explore this connection was Herbert Benson from Harvard. His important book, distributed in the mid-1970s, **The Relaxation Response,** raised a lot of discussions inside intellectual circles. Through medical testing, he showed that changes occurred in the body.

At first, other colleagues were skeptical of his discoveries. Nobody had ever genuinely thought that there could be medical advantages related to this meditative training. In any case, his testing withstood the thorough investigation conducted by others. In the last two decades, mainstream researchers picked up progressively genuine enthusiasm for the subject. The research started, yet more explicitly, the **American Heart Association Journal** published an article that reported the ability of meditation to bring down an individual's risk factors that are associated with all types of cardiovascular illness.

The **American Journal of Hypertension** recently also published positive reviews on the medical advantages of meditation. In this research, it was found that a gathering of meditating people viably brought down their blood pressure, contrasted with a second group that didn't meditate. The decrease in blood pressure for these individuals was so apparent, truth be told, that the meditators had the option to reduce their utilization of antihypertensive drugs by about 25 percent. Stress is related to something beyond coronary illness.

Stress can cause disruption in a lot of physiological functions. At the end of the day, when you're worried all the time, it manifests in the form of any number of medical issues. One of the systems you may have noticed this in is through gastrointestinal dysfunctions. It's not "all in your head," it's been extensively recorded that changes in physiology and hormones happen in your body in relation to stress. These cause various stomach issues, as a response to a distressing condition - either acute or chronic.

A few people also experience sleep disorders due to stress. In some of these cases, sleep issues are linked with irritable bowel syndrome. Fortunately, these physical changes can be reduced and eased through consistent meditation practice.

Meditation Aids Weight Loss

It's hard to be your best when you're troubled with weight issues. Sadly, numerous people who are overweight do not have a good self-image and lack a sense of self-worth. Without that, they may believe that their ideal life is far out of their grasp. Meditation can do something amazing here, in two different ways. To begin with, it's not unusual to start eating when you're stressed out.

If you are someone who does this, you realize that what you go after first is generally something salty, sugary or greasy. It's not about your absence of self-restraint - blame the hormonal changes related to too much stress instead. Your body craves this kind of unhealthy food when it is under distress.

A lot of research demonstrates that the physical impact of stress on your body can be greatly diminished through meditation. It starts by diminishing the body's cortisol level, which can then mitigate those obstinate yearnings for food. Maybe meditating doesn't offer that equivalent comfort that you get from the bag of chips, candy, or fries (or even all three). Yet, it can help curb those cravings in any case. This is a part of the process that will allow people to pick up a superior mental self-image, which, then, empowers them to concentrate on seeking the life that they need to lead. Stress is very slippery. It penetrates your entire being. Maybe, however, its most notable impending impacts are on the person's immunity. Consider it. How often have you caught a cold or even the flu following an unpleasant event?

Meditation can definitely help you with this also. People under pressure are known to have decreased amounts of basic white blood cells, which are essential for battling foreign attacking microscopic organisms and infections, which can cause cold, influenza, and other illnesses. Meditation is undoubtedly now seen as a great way to insightfully deal with the stress in your life.

Meditation Helps Manage Headaches

A headache is one of the most common signs that your body is experiencing too much stress. What's more, it's difficult to concentrate on what is important to you when a headache is floating over the majority of your thoughts. It's hard to think, and at the same time, it's hard to use sound judgment, and it's tough to enjoy yourself. Maybe it doesn't come as anything unexpected that meditation is the ideal method to loosen up those muscles and suppress that pain.

In addition to the fact that it works for most people, its positive effects are likewise scientifically confirmed. Even for a brief timeframe, going within yourself as meditation allows you to make changes in your brain waves to another higher state. This is a dimension of awareness that is known to help advance the process of healing. The takeaway here is that through meditation, you can adjust your brain waves. Researchers were once convinced that an individual's brain waves are unchangeable. They trusted that we are brought into the world with specific patterns, and these couldn't be modified, despite our ability to switch between different dimensions of cognizance.

Today, however, it's broadly acknowledged that your brain waves **can** be changed—and meditation is one way in which this can be accomplished. The most recent studies have taken a look at people who have been meditating for over fifteen years. Long-term meditation changes the functioning of the brain, which permits the individuals who meditate to achieve a more elevated amount of mindfulness than the individuals who don't. In any case, nothing is preventing you right now from disposing of that migraine through a ten-or fifteen-minute session of meditation, so why not try it?

As you can see, meditation has a lot of benefits for those who practice it regularly. There are actually more ways in which it helps than just the ones mentioned above. If you genuinely want to experience the benefits of meditation, you need to get started.

How to establish a Good Meditation Practice?

One effective way to consistently practice meditation is to create and plan out a practice that you can follow, according to your needs, your daily schedule, routines, and timing.

The thing about meditation is that you need to be mindful of everything that you experience in your session. With mindful meditation, there is a goal and a purpose. It is to help you be conscious and mindful of everything you do.

Benefits of Establishing A Meditation Practice

A foundation of your meditation session is important because, in many ways, when you set the stones to your practice, your brain will start moving toward making this practice happen. For example, if you decide to buy a new meditation mat, your mind will be reminded (or you will remember) that you purchased the mat, and you want to know the feeling of sitting on the mat and practicing.

Without a firm foundation, you will not be consistent

It won't be long before whatever you're doing eventually crumbles and falls because there's nothing supporting it. That's just one way of describing how important it is to develop a sound meditation practice right from the very beginning of the process.

It helps you create a habit

But although meditation is something that is beneficial for everyone, not everyone is currently putting it into practice. Some people are not practicing meditation at all. Why? Because it isn't a habit. A lot of us lead very busy lives, so sometimes our plates seem too full to take on anything else. There will always be a reason not to start something, which is why it is entirely up to you to make time for it.

The purpose of establishing a meditation practice is because you want to make meditation a habit, a part of your daily life, and something that you are willing to do every day without even thinking twice or resisting it because you are pressed for time.

It makes your practice ingrained, almost second-nature activity in your life

Meditating will become much like how brushing your teeth or showering, preparing something to eat, and even going on a daily commute to work. Those habits are so deeply ingrained in you that you do them without any effort or a lot of thought put into it.

That is what establishing a meditation practice aims to do for you right now, and it is something you need to establish as a foundation to make your practice consistent.

Here is how you can start establishing a meditation practice for yourself.

- Start small. Start small at first by meditating for short periods of time, maybe 5-10 minutes a day, especially if you're new at it. You can do anything for 5-10 minutes a day with no resistance, and the time will pass before you even know it. When you see how easy that was, it keeps you motivated to keep adding onto that. By creating small, achievable goals, you begin building the habit of making meditation a part of your daily life.

- Use tools to help you. There is an app for just about everything these days, even meditation, so why not make the most of the tools you have to help you establish a successful daily practice? There are several apps, such as Headspace and Calm, which can help you enhance your meditation sessions, with everything from timers to ambient sounds to help set the mood. If it helps make your daily practice more enjoyable, why not? You are more likely to stick to something if you like what you're doing.

- Use YouTube. Guided meditations that you like on YouTube can be a great tool, especially for beginners on this journey. It helps you stay on track and on the right path. Some meditations are given on a daily basis, whereas some are based on your goals, such as Meditation for Focus and Meditation for Sleep. Guided meditations make it much easier for beginners, especially to start getting into the flow of things and helps you progress in the right direction with your meditation sessions, especially when you're doing it alone as a solo practice. It would be good to know that you are heading in the right direction.

- Make space. This is extremely important. Making space in your home or anywhere you feel comfortable is a vital part of your practice.

- Make it a schedule. Okay, so not many people like routine and schedule, but if you are starting in meditation practices, this is essential. Make it a point to pencil it into your calendar or make a note of it on your calendar app on your phone. It can be easy for other things going on during the day to take precedence over your meditation session, which is why you need to purposely make that time just to stop and meditate before the day comes to an end, and you realize you didn't get to spend any time meditating at all.

Chakra Healing Meditation

When healing your chakras, it is important to start at the root and work your way up rather than working from the top down.

Begin by focusing all of your energy at the base of your spine. Breathe in and out as you continue to feel this in your body. Each part of your body should be relaxed in this moment.

Start by making sure that you are not holding on to any tension in your legs or your arms. Our chests and our stomach can also stay rather tight from all the tension. Breathe in as you fill yourself with positivity and breathe out any of the tension that you are still holding within these different parts. Your root chakra is also known as Muladhara.

Your root chakra will deal with different aspects of your career. Money and mindset are also involved in this. Anything that deals with your overall survival will be located within this root chakra. If you are struggling with your career, monetary issues, or anything else that creates the life that you have, then this could be creating a blockage in your root chakra. The worst possible thing for this root chakra is fear.

When you are holding on to that anxiety and stress, no matter what it might be over, then it will be found within the blockage passageways of your root chakra.

Breathe in positivity and allow this part of yourself to become clean. Any part of your overall foundation of life needs to be healed within this moment. Let yourself be as grounded as possible.

Breathe in for one, two, three, four, and five. Breathe out for five, four, three, two, and one.

Become independent from your financial state. This does not determine who you are as a person. Having a lot of money or having no money at all will create a very different lifestyle. The only people who say that money isn't everything are those that already have money. Money can provide you, not with happiness, but with the relief and the security needed in order to actually explore that happiness. What we have to remember is that regardless of our financial state, we are still living, breathing individuals. We still have needs, wants, and desires. There are greater things in life than seeking out money. Of course, you need to have money in order to pay for basic living expenses. But beyond that, we do not need money to provide us with any sort of fulfillment. Let yourself become free from this type of stress.

Remind yourself that work is not everything, either. Many people will believe that their job is their life, but you have so much more to live for aside from just this. Feel at the bottom of your spine and all throughout your legs as your root chakra becomes released. The stress and the fear will only make this worse. Of course, you will not be free from the worry over money, but you do not have to let that panic get to a level where it is causing a blockage of your energy. Breathe in positivity and happiness and breathe out anything that is keeping you restricted here. Let's move up now to our sacral chakra. This is known as your Svadhishthana.

This chakra deals with pleasure. Anything associated with sexuality will be found within this energy center as well.

Your sacral chakra is located in your lower abdomen. You can feel where your belly button is now and know that around two or three inches beneath this is where you will discover your sacral chakra. Anything dealing with your guilt or worry over your relationships, could be found here.

If you have an indulgence, or a lack of pleasure, this could create a certain problem in your life. The desire and seeking of too much pleasure can be a distraction.

Everyone deserves to have fun, but it can quickly become an addiction.

Consider now if you have been over indulgent with anything. Even food could be a form of addiction or release that is helping you to avoid emotional problems you don't want to confront. Feel yourself become released from this now.

Sexuality is another huge part of the energy that makes up your sacral chakra. Have you been experiencing difficulties with your sexual life? Is there a partner that you have been having problems with? Do you feel as though this area of your life is lacking anything substantial? Breathe in positivity and breathe out any of the blockages that are keeping your sacral chakra from having the ability to completely heal. Breathe in and out, in and out. Moving up is our solar plexus chakra. This is referred to as your Manipura.

Your solar plexus chakra deals with your own personal power. Breathe in for one, two, three, four, and five. Breathe out for five, four, three, two, and one.

This is your willpower and the motivation that you have within. Can you be confident and in control of your life? This ability will be discovered within that location on your body. It is essential that we ensure we are not putting any blockages or negativity into our own ability to have this kind of power.

GUIDED SELF-HEALING MEDITATION

This solar plexus chakra is located above your belly button and just below your chest, in the stomach area. This is where you will experience butterflies in your stomach when you know that something is wrong. This is where that big heavy ball will be. When something is making you nervous or giving you an unsteady feeling, then you might discover that pit in your stomach. This is your solar plexus chakra telling you that you need to take control. If you feel any sort of shame over yourself, or embarrassment about who you are, this will be a huge blockage. You cannot properly make positive decisions for yourself when this solar plexus chakra is being blocked. You need to have that belief and that strength in your own abilities so that you can live to your fullest potential.

Breathe in positivity and breathe out anything that has been blocking this part of your body. Your self-worth will also be regulated by the energy that exists here. Your self-esteem is an important part as well and you need to be able to nurture that so that you can make better decisions. Loving yourself and fulfilling your needs of having a high self-esteem is healthy and it does not make you egotistical; we need to check in with ourselves so that we can be our own biggest fan. Breathe in and out. Breathe in self-love and breathe out any of the hate and doubt that has been keeping this part of your chakras blocked.

Moving up we have our heart chakra. This is the chakra that deals with everything involving love and relationships. This energy does not just regulate personal relationships with other people. It is also responsible for helping you control the love that you have for yourself.

Any sort of grief or remorse will be the biggest blockage for this part of your heart chakra. It is located right in between your breasts in that deep part of your chest. It is also known as the Anahata.

Any type of joy or inner peace that you experience will be found in this part of your body. Your heart might beat faster when you are happier. Your heart may be heavy when you are unsure of yourself and you don't know what to do. This will all be part of the regulation of your heart chakra.

Breathe in happiness and breathe out hate. Fill yourself up with peace and let go of any of the grief or shame that you might be feeling. Let yourself heal from the emotional trauma and relationships with romantic people that might have been causing you this sort of blockage. Breathe in positivity and breathe out anything that is keeping you restricted.

Above this is our throat chakra. This is located right in your throat. It is also referred to as Vishuddha. This throat chakra is all about communication. Look at your life now and the way that you have been talking

GUIDED SELF-HEALING MEDITATION

and interacting with other people. Do you share the things that are on your mind? Are you not afraid to stand up for what you know is right and true?

It fills you with hate when you spread that to somebody else. Open your mouth wide now and breathe in as big of a breath as you can. Feel yourself fill with positive air.

Hold it for just a few moments and now exhale as hard as you can, letting go of all of that hate that you have been sending to other people. Feel yourself become lifted and free once you let go of all that toxic energy that is being passed around. Your throat chakra can also be blocked when you are not properly using it. Are you more of a passive person who isn't willing to share what is on their mind? This is only going to keep your throat chakra closed off even more. Open this part of yourself up and let yourself communicate with other people. Breathe in and out, in and out. Let yourself be at peace.

Moving up to the middle of our forehead, we have our third-eye chakra. This is known as your Ajna.

Your third-eye chakra is your intuition. It is something that will help lead you through this life. Not everybody will be able to even tap into their third-eye chakra in their life, even when they already know that it exists. You have to allow yourself to see the truth. Sometimes we know that the truth is right in front of us, but we keep that third-eye closed because we're not ready to look at it. Open this up now and be honest with yourself. Once you relieve this blockage, you will find that every other chakra aligns. Once you stop looking the other way with your third-eye and instead look right in front of you, this is going to help keep your body at peace and bring everything together in perfect harmony.

Breathe in and out, in and out. Your imagination, your creativity, your wisdom, and your logical thinking all exists within this third-eye as well. Any sort of illusion or deceit that you have been experiencing, or even creating on your own, is going to be a huge blockage for this third-eye chakra.

Feel your eyes become open. See the things that are right in front of you. Close your eyes once again and breathe in. You do not have to use your physical set of eyes to really let this third-eye breathe. Let the air travel in and out. Breathe in positivity and truth and breathe out any sort of neglect that you have had over your life.

On top of all of these chakras finally is our crown chakra. This is known as your Sahasrara.

Your crown chakra represents how connected you can be to your spirituality, regardless of whatever you might believe in this life. You have something deeper inside of you that extends beyond just your physical body. Allow this crown chakra to be your guidance. Feel this take power over you and let it be the thing that drives the rest of your chakras. Trust your intuition. Let yourself speak your truth. Feel and spread the love. Trust your gut and know when something is right or wrong. Allow yourself to feel pleasure but remember that it can't be everything. Keep yourself grounded and rooted in this earth and the present moment. The only way that you can heal is after you have managed to clean these out. Think of a physical wound that you might get. If you were to scrape your knee, before putting ointment or a bandage on it to heal, you first need to make sure that it is clean. If you are not properly cleaning something out first, then it could trap something negative or toxic inside of it, which would cause it to spread everywhere else and get even worse than it was before the initial wound.

You have cleaned your chakras, and you have granted yourself the ability to fully heal, breathe in and out, in and out. You are completely at peace; your chakras have aligned, and you know now what it takes to feel at ease. You are relaxed and you are mindful.

You are present in this moment and you are prepared. You are peaceful and serene.

You are now completely relaxed and at ease. You have tapped into every one of your chakras. You know where they exist inside of you now and it is time to start the healing process. You'll be able to go back to this whenever you need to ensure that you don't have any blockages.

This is the perfect beginner and warm-up meditation because it means that you will be able to go through the rest of these meditations with a clear mind and a healthy flow through your body. Continue to focus on your breathing once again. Breathe in for one, two, three, four, and five, and out for five, four, three, two, and one.

Feel yourself already start to heal in this process. Allow your body to become calm and centered.

We are going to count down from twenty once again. When we reach one, you will either drift off to sleep, continue on with your day, or move onto the next meditation.

Chapter Two: Anxiety

Anxiety is a feeling of worry, nervousness or unease about something with an uncertain outcome. You know you are anxious when you feel restless or tensed. Your heart may beat in an accelerated rate and your breathing may quicken. Some people tend to feel tired and weak easily when they are anxious.

It is very important to note and respect the contributions your thoughts make to your anxiety level. Thoughts are the images, memories', beliefs, judgments and reflections that float through your mind and give rise to anxiety. You can ask yourself: "What are the thoughts and images in my mind that keep me feeling as anxious as I feel?"

Meditation has more benefits than just helping us have positive thoughts and thinking, it also rejuvenates our physical and mental health. And often when we help ourselves, we help those around us. In this way, solo meditation can positively affect a relationship.

It is understandable if you feel wary about using meditation to cure your anxiety. You may find it hard to believe that a seated, quiet and isolated activity can help strengthen your social skills, reduce your anxiety level and relationship skills, but research shows it does.

Ways meditation can prevent anxiety in your relationship.

Strained Communication

Communication is essential for a healthy relationship. If the communication in your relationship is strong, then it has the potential of being healthy and lasting.

Meditation will free you from within and any hindrance to your having an effective communication in a relationship, will be easy to deal with.

Toxic Personality

No sane human will want to be found in a relationship with a toxic human. Sometimes, though, the toxicity usually arises as a result of clashes in opposite personalities. You might worry that your personality is causing undue stress on your partner. This worry can cause you a lot of anxiety. You can change your existing scenario with meditation. As a human being, you must have carried your emotional and mental baggage for many years without relieve. Apart from a series of outbursts caused by emotional imbalances, this might even cost you your health. Just like snakes that shed their skin and dogs that shake off water from their fur, you need to shake off the baggage you have carried around before you can successfully rejuvenate yourself. When your mind is free of constant worry, you would find it easy to be happy and, in turn, spread that happiness to others. What you have inside you, is what you would reflect to others around you. This will ease your anxiety and you will find yourself becoming your partners' peace. Your partner will also feel compelled to reciprocate and you would move on in life, a happier and motivated person.

Former Relationship

This is usually a great cause of strained relationships and needless anxiety. Meditation helps you heal from any past heartbreak you might have experienced. During meditation, the mind is content and alert so, it can greatly heal the body, heart and soul. It harmonizes the mind and triggers the healing process.

Gratefulness

A very strong incentive to meditate for a good relationship is its impact on your perspective. Meditation helps you control and regulate your emotions and this power will help you keep a positive perspective. Grateful people are usually more satisfied in their relationships and feel closer to one another.

Staying grateful will help you stay focused and appreciative of your partner's good qualities. Your partner, in turn, will feel appreciated, and the bond you share will be strengthened.

Work-Related Stress

You might be going through and experiencing a lot of stress at work.

It Keeps You Positive

Meditation helps you stay positive, charismatic. It makes you more present, more focused, more productive, and even more creative. Your ability to learn and reason outside the box will improve. It is true that positive emotions help you connect freely with others. It helps us be more open, more approachable and it even solidifies our feelings of connection with other people, even strangers. To explain better: you will realize that on the days you feel anxious and stressed, you are less likely to start up a conversation with the person behind you at a bank. This is because stress makes us selfish and more self-focused. However, though, on the days you feel great, happy and excited, you are more likely to start a conversation or share a joke with a stranger or even notice if someone needs help going through a door.

Research shows that laughter, which only occurs when you are feeling positive, makes you more receptive to new persons and helps you create and strengthen relationships. Also, it helps you endure in the face of difficulty. Difficulty can come in the form of a challenging relationship. All of us will face problems in our relationships, but only some of us have natural resilience and an ability to endure and bounce back quickly. Thousands of researches will show that meditation is a strong way to improve happiness and your general well-being. By helping with anxiety and even depression, it can help keep you in a positive frame of mind that has enormous benefits.

Your Connection

As noted earlier, after a while partners tend to feel disconnected from each other. In a research conducted on loving-kindness and compassion based on meditations, it was realized that these types of meditations can greatly help partners feel more empathetic and connected. Meditation can help train and help you to feel more compassionate and loving. Other research shows that empathy and compassion contribute a lot, positively, to your health, well-being and happiness: improved happiness, decreased anxiety and depression, and even a longer life not to mention stronger and healthier relationships with other persons.

The Five Types of Anxiety Disorders

It is a normal occurrence to be anxious just as mentioned earlier. The way this world works, it would be almost impossible not to have feelings of anxiety repeatedly. We are predisposed to engage ourselves in activities that may give rise to feelings of anxiety: doing exams, asking someone out for a date, making important decisions among others.

Anxiety disorders come in different shapes and forms. The term anxiety disorder only serves as an umbrella term to cover the different conditions under the scope of the term:

Social Phobias (Social Anxiety Disorder)

For socially anxious people, everyday situations can get out of hand in mere seconds. This group of people is extremely self-conscious and fear judgment and scrutiny from other individuals. This phobia links itself to only specific situations:

- Fear of public speaking
- Having meals in front of people

- In extreme cases, others experience it in slight exposure to other people

In the event that you experience these kinds of symptoms, you might actually be suffering from social anxiety.

Generalized Anxiety Disorder (GAD)

Generalized Anxiety Disorder has the tendency of making the victims feel unfounded worry as well as the lingering feeling that something negative is about to happen. Often, these feelings come in excessive proportions and are mostly unrealistic.

Post-Traumatic Stress Disorder (PTSD)

Contrary to popular belief, PTSD does not only affect soldiers and prisoners of war. This anxiety disorder comes about when someone goes through adverse conditions that may terrify or cause physical harm to him or her. A couple of traumatic events can easily lead one to post-traumatic stress disorder: various accidents, natural or synthetic disasters and violence imposed on them. Three symptoms generally characterize PTSD:

- Flashbacks, nightmares, and vivid recollections of the events that lead to the current state.

- Having insomnia coupled with the inability to concentrate as well as amplified feelings of anger and irritation.

- Heavy avoidance of places, things or activities that serve as a constant reminder of the traumatic event.

Panic Disorder

People who suffer from panic disorders always have terror knocking at their doors on a constant. The affected parties also experience sweating, heavy palpitations (usually irregular) and chest pains. In addition, none of these episodes comes with a warning and the fear of another attack only adds the magnitude of the panic. In extreme cases, victims may experience a choking sensation and symptoms that they may be having a heart attack.

Obsessive-Compulsive Disorder (OCD)

When the term OCD comes up, many people often characterize it with the washing of hands and turning on and off lights. However, to many people, many things are a mystery about people who suffer from OCD. OCD has the characteristic of repetitive actions and thought patterns (obsessions) that recur. Some of the obsessions are:

- The fear of contamination from germs
- Unwelcome thoughts of harm, religion, or sex
- Thoughts of aggression towards the self or other parties
- Arranging thing is perfect symmetry

Some of these repetitive actions may be arranging things in a specific way, excessive urge to clean the surroundings and wash hands, counting and checking things repeatedly to confirm if they are in order.

There is no way, for certain, to be able to tell when or how someone will develop an anxiety disorder. Gladly, there are steps present, which can help reduce or alleviate the symptoms. Contained in this book are some of these steps.

Easy Steps to Help You Overcome Anxiety in your Relationship

1. Be Calm

You must have found yourself criticizing everything you do. It is normal, we all have an inner critic in us that thrives in cooking up doubt and filling our minds with anxious thoughts. If this occurs, the very first thing you should strive to do is calm yourself so it doesn't spiral out of control. Meditation calms the nervous system and gives you an opportunity to create separation between you and those negative thought lines. You will come to realize that you do not have to react to every thought that flips into your mind. So, take in some long calming breaths and put aside some good meditation time.

2. Process the Facts

The next step is to figure out the exact negative situation that is making you anxious. This is because, most of the things that make us anxious, are based on thoughts we make up in our own head. So if for any reason, your relationship is causing you anxiety, search yourself and find out why it is and while doing that focus only on facts not opinions. This will help you fully understand your present situation rather than some imagined failure.

3. Self-Care

GUIDED SELF-HEALING MEDITATION

When you begin to feel anxious about your relationships, it is necessary to concentrate on taking good care of yourself. Instead of acting out against your partner or trying to get reassurance, do only those things that will promote your wellbeing and make you feel confident.

4. Heal from Within

You would have noticed by now that these steps are all the necessary steps you need to take to gain control over yourself and definitely not your partner. Heal yourself from within, this is really the only way you can cope with these potentially harmful feelings, because they come from within. It is possible to worry and be aware of yourself without being anxious.

5. Mindfulness-Based Meditation

Meditation used to effectively treat anxiety disorders usually comes in the form of Mindfulness-Based Meditation. This form of meditation can be dutifully traced to the mindfulness movement started by Jon Kabat-Zinn who is the founder of the Mindfulness-Based Stress Reduction Approach. The simple aim of the Mindfulness-Based Stress Reduction Approach is to learn to completely avoid troubling thoughts. You can achieve this by practicing awareness, figuring out the cause of anxiety in your body, knowing your thought process and learning how best to do away with your painful emotions.

MBSR works better when practiced with an instructor, but you can achieve the same result from courses available online.

Steps for Mindfulness Meditation to Distill Relationship Anxiety

Below are easy steps to follow to get started today:

1. Sit upright in a chair with the palms of your feet flat on the floor.

2. Focus on your breath. Pay attention to your breathing. Do not try to vary how you are breathing, just watch and observe your body as you breathe in and out.

3. You might get distracted or find that you want to focus on something else. Ignore and defiantly resist this longing and continue to concentrate on your breathing.

4. Anxious thoughts may at this point, cross your mind. It is expected. Do not shut them down

rather, acknowledge them and then calmly go back to awareness of your breathing.

5. Keep up with this calm, non-critiqued observation for close to ten minutes.

6. Slowly open your eyes and take note of how you feel. Don not try to analyse the feeling, just observe.

It is easy to practice meditation. All you have to do is accept the world, the environment around you. Be curious. Observe. This meditative practice, after a while, will spill into other parts of your life, as you concentrate on yourself observing rather than focusing on anxious and difficult situations and over-reacting.

Difficulties in This Meditation

There are several detractors to meditations. You might find that it is hard to meditate or be mindful. You might find it difficult to concentrate without letting the critique voice speak or you may feel too busy or restless as though there is simply too much to do, to be lounging around, breathing in and out. People are wired differently. Some people simply find it difficult to just do nothing. They are constantly on the move and they are used to it. Also, sometimes, you might realize that you cannot prevent the difficult thoughts from taking over even when you try to relax.

The best advice that will help to overcome these obstacles comes in two ways:

Respect the process

You should understand and recognize that this will take some time. You will not become an expert at this in a day. When you first start meditating, you will feel strange. Your mind will bug you, make you feel that you are wasting your time, just sitting around there doing nothing literal. You will get even get angry and fed up. Even with all this, though, religiously continue with it. It will definitely get better. Do not expect your very first meditation practice to be easy at all, it may not. Funny as it sounds, it does take practice to master the art of doing absolutely nothing. In the end, it will become easier.

Create time

Since you have identified the fact that the Meditation will take time, it is best to make out time for it. Put in a time for it on your schedule just like you put in a job or an appointment. Do not make it an option not to practice. There is no reason why practice should be skipped for a day. Just discipline yourself. Tell yourself that you need to get it done. Most times, when you find that you have got a lot of things to do and achieve and you still try to fit in time for a calm moment, you will discover, later, that that calm moment helped you to go back to your day more aware and faster at solving problems.

Update a diary with records on your growth and truthfully indicate if your anxiety is reducing. After a short while of constant meditation, you should ask yourself questions like: When anxious thoughts flashed through your mind, were you able to examine them without criticizing or judging them? Did you succeed in acquiring a moment of focused observation? Did you feel calm, relaxed and aware? If after a while, you are still plagued with troubling thoughts and anxiety that is repetitive and harsh, go ahead and have a talk with your doctor about other treatment options.

How to Practice Meditation for GAD

If you are suffering from Generalized Anxiety, mentioned earlier, performing constant daily meditation can assist you in overcoming anxiety and in reducing increased tension in your body. Yoga has a lot to do with meditation so If you have ever taken a yoga class, you have taken a good first step and you are already on the right path to achieving the peace you seek.

Again, at first, you will not need a whole lot of time to meditate. A few minutes may be a you need. Make efforts to make out a few minutes each day to meditate. As you become more and more familiar with the process, and as you figure out how to relax and discover what it feels like to be calm, you can slowly increase that time.

GAD is simply unrelenting worry, worry that would not go away. Meditation helps you to learn to live with those worries and thoughts without giving them the power to upset you. When you finally achieve that, your distress is more likely to reduce.

Chapter Three: How To Calm The Body

Exercise

Exercise is a highly recommended stress reliever for many reasons. Physical activity has many benefits in addition to reducing stress, and these benefits alone (increased health, longevity, and happiness) make exercise a worthwhile habit. And as a stress management technique, it is more effective than others. The combined benefits of these two facts make physical exercise a lifestyle that is worth following.

Do physical activity

The definition of physical activity in this context has not been limited only to exercise. Physical activity is any activity that engages your physique. Mostly it will lead to perspiration. When an individual engages in physical activity, he or she is obliged to concentrate fully on that particular activity. Exercising is a very renowned way to counter depression. Regular exercise has time and again been used as an anti-depressant. When one is exercising, endorphins are boosted. These are chemicals that enable an individual to feel good.

The statistics of how many people deal with stress is always on the upward. When one experiences stress, it has a lasting effect in their lives since it cuts across what an individual is engaging in at a particular time. To eradicate stress completely is an uphill task, and one would rather manage it. Exercising is one of the best methods to manage stress. Many medical practitioners advise that individuals should engage in exercises in a bid to manage stress levels.

The advantages that come with a person engaging in exercises have far been established to be a counter-measure against diseases and as a method of enhancing the body's physical state. Research has it that exercising helps a great deal when decreasing fatigue and enhancing the body's consciousness of the environment. Stress invades the whole of your body, affecting both the body and mind. When this happens, the act of your mind feeling well will be pegged on the act of the body feeling well too. When one is in the act of exercising, the brain produces endorphins that act naturally as pain relievers. They also improve the instances upon which an individual falls asleep. When the body is able to rest, this means that its amounts of anxiety have dropped by a large margin. Production of endorphins can also be triggered by the following practices. They include but are not limited to meditation and breathing deeply. Participation in exercise regularly has proven an overall tension reliever.

Doing relaxation exercises

Another method of reducing stress levels is through the use of some relaxation techniques. A relaxation technique is any procedure that is of aid to an individual when trying to calm down the levels of anxiety. Stress is effectively conquered when the body itself is responding naturally to the stress levels in the body. Relaxation can be often confused with laying on a couch after a hard day. This relaxation is best done in the form of self-meditation, although its effects are not fulfilling on the impact of stress. Most relaxation techniques are done at the convenience of your home with only an app.

The following types of exercise are highly recommended for stress reduction because they have specific properties that are effective in reducing stress in short and long-term stress management:

Yoga

The gentle stretching and balance of yoga may be what people think when they practice, but there are several other aspects of yoga that help reduce stress and to have a healthy life. Yoga entails the same type of diaphragmatic breathing; this is used with meditation. In fact, a few yoga styles include meditation as part of their practice (in fact, most types of yoga can take you to some degree of meditation).

Yoga also includes balance, coordination, stretching, and styles are the exercise of power. All support health and stress reduction. Yoga can be practiced in many ways. Some yoga styles feel like a gentle massage from the inside, while others sweat and hurt you the next day, so there is a yoga school that can work for most people, even for those who have some physical limitations, to be attractive.

Walking

Walking is one of the easiest medications to relieve stress that is excellent because of the benefits this technique offers. The human body was designed to travel long distances, and this activity generally did not cause as much wear as it did. Walking is an exercise that can be easily separated by the speed you use, the weights you carry, the music you listen to, and the location and the company you choose.

This type of exercise can also be easily divided into 10 minutes of sessions, and classes are not needed, and no special equipment is needed beyond a good pair of shoes. (This is an advantage since studies have shown that three 10-minute workouts provide the same benefits as a 30-minute session: great news for those who, due to their busy schedule, need to practice in parts! To find the More smalls!)

Martial Arts

There are many forms of martial arts, and although each one may have little focus, ideology, or set of techniques, they all have benefits to relieve stress. These practices tend to pack both aerobic and strength training, as well as the confidence that comes from physical and self-defense skills.

Generally practiced in groups, martial arts can also offer some of the benefits of social support, as classmates encourage each other and maintain a sense of group interaction. Many martial arts styles provide philosophical views that promote stress management and peaceful life, which you can choose or not accept. However, some styles, especially those with high levels of physical combat, have a higher risk of injury, so martial arts are not for everyone, or at least not all styles work for everyone. If you try several different martial arts programs and talk to your doctor before following the style, you have a better chance of finding a new habit that keeps you fit for decades.

These three examples are not the only types of exercise. They simply show some benefits and are usable by most people. There are many other forms of workout that can be very powerful, such as Pilates, running, weight training, swimming, dancing, and prepared sports.

Everyone brings their stress management benefits to the table, so discover and practice the form of exercise that appeals to you the most.

Mindfulness Body Scan Meditation

This technique requires a more formal atmosphere than the breathing technique as it is best experienced when you are lying down or sitting in a really comfortable posture. While lying down may seem like a fabulous way, initially, it might not be a good idea in the long-run because novices tend to fall asleep in this position. Also, while a good 30-minute duration is needed for effective results, you may make the best use with whatever little time you get.

Sit down on a cushion or a chair or lie down comfortably on the floor. Avoid lying on a mattress if you find it difficult to stay awake. Close your eyes because it makes it easy to focus. Now, pay attention to your breath. Slowly move your attention to the places where your body is in contact with your chair or floor. Investigate each section of your body mentally.

The different sensations you experience could be tingling, pressure, tightness, temperature, or anything else. Sometimes, you may not feel any sensation too. Notice the absence of sensations also. Each section of your body becomes an anchor for your mind to hold on so that it doesn't wander away.

Again, be aware when your mind wanders, and gently get it back to where it was before it moved off. When you are done, open your eyes, and mindfully get your focus back on the outside environment.

Another crucial aspect of the body scan mindfulness technique is to release the tension in the various parts of your body as you scan it. When you focus on a particular section of the body, say your shoulders, you suddenly realize that you are holding them too rigid and creating tension in that area. By focusing on that part, tension is automatically released from there.

These are formal ways of body scans and breathing mindfulness meditation techniques. You can do these mindfulness activities even while sitting in your chair in your office. Take a 5-minute break and do a body scan or focus on your breath even as you sit at your desk. You don't even have to get up from your seat. Also, you could do it during your daily commute or while waiting for someone or standing in line for something or anywhere else. Mindfulness meditation does not need anything else but your mind, which is always with you.

Mindfulness Meditation through Mantra Chanting

A mantra is a phrase, word, or syllable that is repeated during the meditation session. Mantras can be repeated in mind, whispered, or chanted aloud. Mantra meditation involves two elements, including the mantra that is being chanted and mindfulness meditation using the mantra as the anchor. Mantra chanting keeps the mind focused and facilitates mindfulness meditation. People also use the mantra as a form of positive affirmations.

Identify the best mantra for your needs. You can choose your mantra based on the reason for the mantra chanting. Are you looking at getting back your health? Are you seeking peace? Do you desire for something to happen in your life? Are you looking for a deep spiritual awakening?

Sit comfortably with your back straight but not rigidly erect. Focus on your breathing first, which will help you get into the mindfulness meditation state. Ensure your intention for the mantra chanting and meditation is clearly imbibed in your mind. Now, start chanting the mantra. Don't expect miracles when you start your chant. Simply repeat the mantra slowly, deliberately, and in a relaxed manner. In this mindfulness meditation technique, mantras are the anchors that help your mind to focus.

There are no 'best' mantras for mindfulness meditation. You can choose anything from the scriptures of your personal religion, or you can choose positive and empowering affirmations such as:

- I am happy and content at this moment.
- All my treasures are inside of me.
- My heart is my best guide.
- It's always now.
- I am complete, and I don't need anything outside of me to make me whole.
- Nothing is permanent.
- This too shall pass.

Breathing Exercises throughout the Day

Breathing is a fundamental principle of our lives. You must breathe in and out to live. Many times, people suffer from breathing-related problems, which later on affect them. Some have lost their dear lives because of having difficulties in breathing. Others are suffering because they are unable to breathe well. Therefore, it is essential to note the exact significance of breath.

The first important of breathing is that it reduces anxiety. Breathing also helps in the elimination of insomnia. It has the power to manage your day to day cravings, and also it can control and manage your anger response. Breathing brings your whole body into more excellent balance as it can initiate calmness within you. You will realize your entire being becomes normal again after a proper process of breathing and level of stress will be no more. For those having a high level of emotional frustrations can also apply breathing techniques all through the day so that they might get well too. Nothing is as sweet and pleasant as having an excellent relaxed body.

Breathing also aids in other functions within your bodies, such as muscle relaxation, digestion, and even peristalsis processes. The movement of fluids within your body is made possible by the help of breathing. Breathing helps in the transportation of your body elements such as nutrients and oxygen. It also aids in the removal of waste products. It is better to note that breathing has got that most considerable impact on your respiration as it can donate the required oxygen for respiration. You can acquire the exact energy needed for normal body functions. You will feel strong because power has been formed in your body tissue. Your muscles will be stable since the energy to undertake all your body functions are there. Therefore, you will realize that breathing is a continuous and dynamic process that has no end. Throughout the day, you will understand that breath is an incurring process. The first breathing technique that you will realize is part and parcel of your whole day is reducing stress through ***breathing.*** Before doing this breathing process, try as much as possible to adopt a good sitting position. The position should be comfortable and relaxing. You can also place your tongue behind your front upper teeth and do the following:

1. Start by making sure your lungs are empty. You can do this by allowing the air inside to escape through your nose and mouth. You can facilitate this process by doing some enlargement of your shoulder and chest and contracting your stomach so that you increase the exhale process.

2. Now you can breathe in through your nose. It should be tranquil and silent. Remember, it is supposed to take only 4 seconds.

3. The next step is to hold your breath, let's say for about 7 seconds. Don't rush here as your breath should just come naturally.

4. Then go ahead by breathing out. You have to force all air out through your mouth. You can purse your lips too and making some sounds of your preference. This should take at least 8 seconds.

5. Repeat this process four times.

Therefore, this breathing technique to delete stress in life is seen as a formidable way to control anxiety. Therefore, your level of anxiety will reduce. You will start having a perfect life without stress and anxiety. Remember, this process takes time. It is now recommended that you perform it in a sitting position that's not only affordable but also comfortable. This type of breathing is the famous 4-7-8 breathing.

The next breathing technique that you can efficiently perform is belly breathing. Belly breathing is not difficult to implement. It is among the most straightforward breathing techniques that can eventually help you to release stress. The following steps are deemed appropriate for your breathing.

1. Look for a sitting posture or lie flat in any way as far as it is comfortable.

2. Place your hands on both your belly and chest, respectively. Remember to put one and just below the rib cage.

3. Now you can start breathing. Take an intense breath through your nose and let your hand be pushed out of its position by the belly. The other hand should not move even an inch.

4. The next step is to breathe out very loud and produce that whistling sound with your pursed

lips. You can feel that palm on your belly moves in as it pushes out the air.

5. You are allowed to repeat this process more than ten times and make sure to take your time with every single breathing you are undertaking.

6. Remember to make a note on your feelings at the end of the whole process.

Therefore, belly breathing is a type of breathing that will help you to reduce tension within your stomach tissues. Your chest tissues and even your ribs will feel relaxed. In the end, the anxiety within your body decreases, and your calmness comes back to normal.

We also have roll breathing that you can eventually use to delete some sorts of anxiety, stress, depression, and even unpleasant feeling within you. Roll breathing has several important in your body. Roll breathing enlarges your lungs and, as a result, makes you be able to pay a close watch on your breathing. The rhyming and rhythm of your breath become your full focus. You can undertake this breathing anytime and anywhere. However, as a learner, you should use your back on the ground with your legs bent. Then start by doing the following:

- Place your two hands on your belly and chest, respectively. Take a note on the movement of your hands as you concentrate on your breathing process. Continue breathing in and out.

- Focus on filling the lower lungs so that your belly moves up when you are inhaling while your chest does not move an inch. It is better to note that breathing in should be through your nose while breathing out must be through your mouth. You are allowed to repeat this process even ten times so that you can realize better results.

- After filling and emptying your lungs, you can now perform the other step of filling your upper chest. You can manage this by first inhaling in your lower lungs then increasing the tempo so that it reaches the chest. Here, you should breathe regularly but slowly for quite sometimes. During this process, note the position of your two hands. One placed at the belly will slightly fall as the stomach contract. The one put on your chest will rise as more air is breathed in your chest.

- It is now your time to exhale. Go ahead by exhaling slowly through your mouth. You should make that whooshing sound when your hands start falling, respectively. Always, your left hand will have to fall first, followed by your right hand. Still, on this, notice the way tension leaves your body as your mind becomes relaxed and calmed.

- Repeat the whole process of breathing in and out for at least 3 to 5 minutes. In this case, make sure you are observing the movement of your chest and belly. Take note of the rolling wave's motion.

- Your feeling matters a lot in the whole process. Take a more exceptional look at how you feel in the entire rolling breathing.

Your body regains its full free state, and you will feel more relaxed. You can, therefore, practice this rolling breathing process daily and make sure this goes for several weeks. By doing so, you will be able to perform this kind of breathing exercise everywhere. Also, you can eventually achieve this instantly on most occasions. It will help you regain your relaxation and calmness back. At the end of rolling breathing, your anxiety will be at bay. However, this process is not for everyone since some may feel dizzy during the exercise. You can reduce the breathing speed and accelerate slowly. You can then get up slowly after feeling relaxed, calmed, and lightheaded.

Another breathing technique is ***morning breathing***. When you wake up, your body is still exhausted and tired. You feel that your muscles are still weak and wholly tensed. You will realize that your stiffness has got an impact on your day to day activities. The best breathing exercise to follow here is the morning breathing process. It can clear any clogged breathing passages. You can use this method throughout the day to remove the back tension that may be a nagging and a worrying issue to you. The following steps will eventually help you to perform this task with much ease and less effort.

- Stand still and then try to bend forward. You should slightly bend your knees, and your hands should closely dangle on the floor or close to it.

- Start inhaling and slowly exhaling, followed by a deep breath as you return into a standing position. You can roll upward slowly and making sure that your head comes last from the ground.

- Take your time and hold your breath, whether for five seconds or even for 10 seconds. You should do this in your standing position.

- Start exhaling. That is, breathing out slowly while trying to make a return to your initial position. You can bend forward a little bit.

GUIDED SELF-HEALING MEDITATION

- Take note of your feelings at the end of the exercise.

The most important thing about this breathing exercise is that it has the power to instill in you more energy, thus enabling you to carry on with every task of the day. You will be relaxed and calm. The level of anxiousness will reduce. In the end, you will feel more lightheaded and entirely energetic.

The next breathing exercise throughout the day can also involve ***skull shining breath***. The skull shining breath is also known as kapalabhati in another language where the term initially originated. It is a dominant type of breathing that enables you to acquire a relaxed and calm mind and brain. It always boasts of the right way of killing the anxiety in you by eliminating the tension, especially in your skull. Remember, it is good to note that the pressure of the head can negatively influence your whole day, and the impact can remain with you for long.

Skull shining breath is not difficult to undertake, and this will give you that morale of even performing it throughout the day. You can start by having long breathing in then follow it with a quick and extremely powerful breathing out. Exhaling should originate from your belly, especially the lower part.

However, after getting familiarized with the whole contraction process, you can now start on inhaling and exhaling at a faster rate. Increase your pace here and make sure all the breathing process takes place through the nose. In this process, do not involve your mouth at the initial stages. You can go on with the process repeatedly until you start feeling very much relaxed.

You can now take note of your feelings at the end of the breathing exercise. Remember, this breathing process can eventually prevent muscle tension too. It also helps in releasing abdominal pain. Your worries, stress, anxiety, and even clogged breathing sites will be well.

Breathe Deep

Throughout any day, there are bound to be things that cause your stress levels to rise slightly. There are also going to be thoughts that pop into your head and cause you to feel anxious. Our mind can be our own worst enemy, but the good news is we can take control. There are many ways that we can help ease our fears, and deep breathing is one of them!

These techniques are extremely easy to do and can be done anywhere, even at your desk or on the bus to work! If you find it hard to concentrate, you can also purchase a guided relaxation tape, or download a stress-relieving app, as these will guide you through breathing exercises until you get the hang of doing them yourself.

GUIDED SELF-HEALING MEDITATION

Try this:

- Close your eyes and breathe in through your nose for a count of five, hold it for five, and then exhale through your mouth for five, in a slow and controlled manner. Repeat that for as long as you need to gain control.

- Once you're feeling a little calmer or in control, picture the thing that is causing you stress or anxiety as an item or a color. For instance, it might be a black ball, or it might be a gray cloud. It doesn't matter what it is; it simply needs to symbolize the thing that is negatively affecting your day.

- Now, visualize yourself forcefully pushing that item far away from you, and visualize it disappearing into the distance.

- Finish off with the same breathing technique you started with, before gently coming back into the room.

This is a method you can use for any type of stress or anxiety that is bothering you, and it's a great way to get rid of an issue that is upsetting you at any stage during the day.

Another essential breathing technique is ensuring that we are taking deep, full breaths. When we are even the slightest bit stressed, we start breathing shallowly. These shallow, short breaths do not give us enough oxygen and can even lead to full-blown panic attacks. To stop poor breathing, place your hand an inch or two above your stomach. Now, slowly breathe in through your nose until your stomach touches your hand. Go with our usual 5 counts inhales, and hold for a few seconds before slowly exhaling out through your mouth.

When our breathing is shallow, we only fill up the top portion of our lungs with air. Placing your hand above your stomach ensures that you are breathing deeply enough where your entire lungs are filled!

Deep breathing is the foundation of many calming strategies. It can be done on its own or with other methods like meditation, tai chi yoga, etc. Deep breathing is easy because we need to breathe to remain alive, but strongly and efficiently for mental relaxation and stress reduction. Deep breathing focuses on breathing the stomach thoroughly and clean singly. It is easy to learn that you can do it anywhere, and it regulates your stress levels. Sit down with your back straight, inhale through the nose as the belly grows. Inhale as much clean air as possible into the lungs. It makes it possible to get more oxygen into the blood. Exhale the mouth as the belly drops to force as much air as possible out and close the abdominal tract. If you find it difficult to do this sitting, first try

GUIDED SELF-HEALING MEDITATION

to lie down. You could put your hands on your chest and stomach to see if it's wrong.

Chapter Four: How To Calm The Mind

The world we live in today is a truly beautiful place to be. We may have heard many people say things like "this is a great time to be alive," and they would not be wrong. Limitless opportunities abound around us. Ranging from being able to study to have the careers we have always dreamt of and get our dream jobs to be able to buy the things we want and travel as often as we desire, the world has so much to offer us.

Technology is also a huge part of this mix, as digital communication and social media have made it unnecessary for us to be alone. You can shop online whenever you feel like it, and you can play virtual games and immerse yourself in virtual reality at the click of a button. All these have contributed to making the world a global village that truly runs 24 hours, 7 days a week.

Due to this, we are now expected to spend every part of our days actively working to better our lives. Having some downtime is no longer considered necessary, and in some cases, you could be viewed as lazy for requesting downtime. This is both a good thing and a bad thing.

GUIDED SELF-HEALING MEDITATION

On the one hand, we are reaping the dividends of how active our society is, on the other hand, we need to consider the toll it is taking on us.

Our brains, just like computers, are not designed to be active all the time. Apart from sleeping at night (which some people do not even take seriously), there is still a lot we can benefit from taking some time to calm our minds and to relax during working hours.

If you are battling with anxiety, you actually need that downtime. You need to unplug from the continuous demands on your time and your mind and calm your mind. Doing this would change and improve the quality of your life.

Why You Should Calm Your Mind

1. More clear reasoning

Indeed, it feels great to have the ability to overcome our issues every day. However, at times, the sheer volume of the choices you make can lead to befuddled reasoning and slanted points of view. Clearing the mind of messiness and dispensing with superfluous interruptions will enable you to focus. In a relaxed state, you can settle on better choices, dodge errors and function with greater mental lucidity.

Setting aside time to calm your mind, using meditation or mindfulness procedures, can assist you with seeing a clearer way through life's difficulties. Unwinding will empower you to place issues in perspective and to prioritize.

2. Guard your heart

It is presently notable that anxiety can greatly increase your risk of hypertension, cardiovascular failures, and other heart issues. There are researches to show that stress and anxiety can lead to a whole lot of health problems that are heart-related. If you want to live longer and protect your heart, you should make out time to calm your mind.

Drawn out times of stress and anxiety cause hormones to be discharged in the body that influences how the heart functions. This can cause long haul harm if not tended to. Serious anxiety can trigger such a great amount of adrenaline to be discharged that an individual can experience symptoms of a heart attack like palpitations or even have a physical cardiovascular breakdown.

Finding a way to diminish and handle anxiety by figuring out how to calm your mind is vital to taking care of the heart.

3. Battling ailments

It is common knowledge that people appear to capitulate to more ailments – colds, tummy bugs, coughs, and sore throats – when they feel anxious or exhausted.

Increased stress and anxiety will cause you to succumb to colds, cases of flu, and other infections. This is because your immune system is affected when you are stressed. As such, your immune system cannot really fight infections the way it should.

If you wind up continually fending off infections or you appear to catch every infection that is around you, decreasing your feelings of anxiety could help. Figuring out how to viably calm your mind is critical to decreasing pressure and could empower you to lead a progressively profitable and more beneficial life – which thusly breaks the cycle of stress and anxiety, which adds to your sicknesses.

4. Fight against depression and anxiety

The World Health Organization estimates that 350 million people all over the world experience the ill effects of depression. Depression and anxiety are presently the leading sources of disability. Specialists in the field feel that it is no happenstance that the rates at which people struggle with depression and anxiety have grown comparatively with their stress levels. These can all be blamed on not taking time to relax and calm your mind.

As well as making your life feel unsavory, uneasiness can genuinely influence your ability to work. Ordinary day by day choices and assignments may feel inconceivable. You may quit taking propane care of yourself and other people under your care, and going to work or even going outside your home might become very difficult for you.

It is important that you protect yourself from these weakening mental conditions, particularly if there is a medical history of either. It is winding up progressively evident that figuring out how to calm your mind is the best technique for mitigating stress and anxiety.

5. Help with weight loss

A growing number of people are becoming overweight or obese. It is getting increasingly obvious that weight has a direct connection to numerous medical issues, such as diabetes, heart disease, cancer, and strokes. It is crucial to your wellbeing that you can maintain healthy body weight.

GUIDED SELF-HEALING MEDITATION

When you cannot calm your mind, your feelings of anxiety grow. Stress causes a hormone called cortisol to be discharged into the circulatory system, and this builds the craving to eat more. This is the reason a considerable lot of people engage in "comfort eating." As well as increase your appetite, it has been indicated that cortisol makes you go after unhealthy foods – foods high in fat and sugar. Foods in this category are considerably bound to make you heap on the pounds.

Setting aside some time to calm your mind can assist you with keeping your body within the healthy weight range for it. Not only will relaxing diminish the measure of comfort eating you take part in, but it will also assist you with seeing the situation with greater lucidity. Lucidity empowers you to design your weight control plans all the more adequately and address your negative dietary patterns.

Calming your mind has numerous advantages – both physical and mental. Your bustling life can make it easy for you to disregard the significance of 'rest' and having the choice to calm your mind. However, it is winding up progressively evident that figuring out how to quiet down and unwind appropriately can help you live a longer and more joyful life. Make it your priority to become familiar with this imperative fundamental ability and set yourself up to receive the numerous rewards.

How to Calm Your Mind through Meditation

1. Alternate Nostril Breathing

Use your left thumb to hold down your left nostril and breathe in through your right nostril. At that point, close your right nostril with your left forefinger, so both are shut, and hold the breath. Release your left nostril alone and breathe out.

With your right nostril still shut, breathe in through your left. Then close your left nostril with your thumb, so the two nostrils are shut, and hold the breath. Now, take your index finger off your right nostril and breathe out.

This is one set. Complete at least five sets to put the left and right right sides of your brain in harmony, quiet your nervous system, and create a sense of calm.

2. The 100-Breaths Method

Close your eyes. Feel your back against your seat, and your feet squeezed immovably on the ground, at that point delicately carry yourself into the present moment. Then start breathing through both nostrils and count as you go on breathing m, thinking "and" for each breathe in, and the number for each breathe out—breathe in "and," breathe out "one"; breathe in "and," breathe out "two."

Feel your tummy rude with every inward breath, and let the breaths reduce as you count yourself into a greater feeling of calm. After you arrive at 100, open your eyes, move your fingers and toes, and bow your head in appreciation for the psychological space you created internally.

3. Full Body Breath Sweep

Start by breathing in through your nose, extending your stomach, and counting to five. As you take in a breath, imagine calming warm light filling your feet, and after that breathe out through your lips at the count of five while envisioning yourself discharging any pressure you may have been holding in there.

Rehash this procedure for your lower legs, your shins, your knees, etc., as far as possible up to your head. After you wrap up your whole body, you'll likely feel lighter, more settled, and calmer.

4. Lip-Touching Breathing

When stirred, your sympathetic nervous system places you in a condition of high alert—that feeling of fight or flight alarm that lets you know there's a type of risk. Your parasympathetic nervous system, when stimulated, produces the contrary inclination—a feeling of relaxation and calmness.

The lips contain parasympathetic nerve strands, making this a basic way to deal with creating a feeling of calm that you can utilize anywhere, whenever. To receive the rewards, you should simply put your lips together, inhale gradually, and say to yourself, "I am calm."

5. Strolling meditation

In spite of the fact that you can do this whenever you're strolling, you might need to locate a serene spot to walk, away from groups, confusion, or noise pollution. If it is a sheltered space, you can walk barefoot. This will give you a feeling of being increasingly connected to the earth.

Remain with your spine straight, with your shoulders and arms lose, and take a couple of inward breaths and exhalations to take in calming energy and inhale out strain.

Then start gradually moving forward and match your breathing with your motion—right foot, breathe in, left foot, breathe out. Utilize the majority of your faculties to completely experience where you are—the warm feeling of sun all over, the delicate sound of wind stirring leaves on trees. The objective isn't to land at a destination; it's basically to be present in the experience of strolling.

6. Meditative bath

It's quite easy to relinquish every other idea when you're standing under a flood of water, set to the ideal temperature for you.

Set aside this time to tune into your faculties. Pick a soap or shower gel you love so that fragrance is intoxicating. Appreciate the feeling of the water on your skin, and feel it dribble down your back, your calves, and your heels.

Notice when you start thinking of the day ahead (or behind you). Try not to pass judgment on the thoughts or yourself for having them. Rather, imagine them going down the drain and afterward take your concentration back to the experience of cleansing your body and mind.

7. Task meditation

Regardless of whether you're vacuuming, cleaning, or washing dishes, it very well may be your meditation time if you immerse yourself totally in action.

Washing dishes, for instance, can be both fulfilling and calming. Feel the warm water on your hands; let yourself appreciate the experience of making something grimy clean once more. Try not to consider completing or what you'll do when you're done. Concentrate exclusively on the doing and check whether you can discover a feeling of acknowledgment and calmness in doing it gradually and well.

8. Mindful Eating

Rather than eating rapidly with one eye on your food and the other on your phone, transform supper time into meditation time. It doesn't take long to eat, so why not set everything aside and set aside this time for yourself? Your mails, messages, and social media pages will still be there when you're done.

Inhale deeply and attempt to recognize the various subtleties of aroma in everything on your plate. At the point when you're eating, take full breaths between each nibble, and consider your meal like a foodie, valuing the various flavors and textures.

If you discover your thoughts meandering to things you've done or need to do, draw your thoughts to the feeling of the fork in your hand. Then inhale deeply, take a bite, and concentrate on relishing the food before you.

Through Mindfulness

Mindfulness transcends meditation. While meditation can be helpful for helping you become more in tune with the workings of your mind, you can reap the benefits of a calm mind through mindfulness.

By simply focusing more on seemingly small details of your life through mindfulness, you can find greater happiness and fulfillment in your life. Better still, you can find that calmness of mind you need to help you deal with anxiety. Below are some ways to calm your mind through mindfulness.

1. Develop a mindfulness mantra.

Mantras help you remember the important things. They can be useful for mindfulness and calming your mind. A useful mindfulness mantra to help with having a calm mind should be one that reminds you to stay in the moment. It could help if your mindfulness mantra draws your attention to the fact that every day is a new day, and you have the option to start afresh and stay connected with the present moment while separating yourself from the worries in your mind.

2. Give yourself a reminder that you are not your thoughts.

Whenever a negative thought crosses your mind, simply identify it as merely a thought and move on. Thoughts are like birds; do not allow the ones you do not want to build a nest in your head. Let them keep flying. You are not that feeling of regret or self-doubt; you are not that feeling of anger or scorn. Consciously separate your personality from your thoughts in your mind.

3. Acknowledge that thoughts emerge normally.

If you cannot change them, then try working to supplant them with other "better" thoughts. Try not to pummel yourself over something you cannot control, but do not overlook them either; basically move past them and decide not to relate to them, even as they cloud your mind.

4. Relax.

GUIDED SELF-HEALING MEDITATION

Take a long breath through your nose and exhale it through your mouth. This can calm you and remind you that your thoughts are a little piece of the boundlessly immense world around you.

5. Thank somebody in any capacity you can.

Indeed, even the little act of saying "thank you" to a waitress or salesperson or receptionist can reconnect you with the present minute, and it can also keep you from getting to be stuck in your own musings, which prevent you from appreciating life as it comes.

6. Grin at a stranger.

Grinning or smiling helps you concentrate outward to the individuals around you, and by reconnecting with this appreciation for other people, you can connect much better to the present minute and remind yourself just to be.

7. Take a walk in the nature.

Take a walk and blend into the earth around you, and tune in for sounds you would generally have missed.

8. Keep a daily gratitude diary.

Keeping an appreciation diary helps pull you away from the pressure of the day. It also constrains you to acknowledge life as it comes and helps you see the positive qualities in life consistently.

9. Leave your telephone on silent throughout the day.

You can also mute your phone's notifications, as these can be diverting and pull you away from the present moment. Your messages will, in any case, be hanging tight for you there later when you are all set to go through them.

Muting your ringer can also prevent every disturbance from obstructing your mind and preventing you from experiencing the genuine feelings of calm you could be having for the duration of the day.

10. Eat gradually.

Concentrating on the look and the taste of what you eat can help remind you that while all feelings are transient, it is essential to genuinely encounter them properly, as opposed to giving them a chance to pass you by.

GUIDED SELF-HEALING MEDITATION

11. Drink tea.

Tea can help quiet your nerves and cleanse your thoughts and connect you more to the present moment.

12. Wash up.

Showers can assist you with unwinding by compelling you to make a cross over from the clamor of the day, and they can be an incredible method to give your stressors a chance to fall away as they blend into the warmth of the water.

13. Tune in to instrumental music.

It has been shown to support your capacity to focus, which can raise your strength and quality of your mind and help you calm down when your thoughts would not quit coming.

14. Handle one of the most stressful things on your plan for the day.

While it is imperative to be mindful irrespective of the demands of your day, do not abstain from finishing a strenuous assignment on your downtime if it is giving you unneeded anxiety.

15. Have a profound discussion with someone you know.

Completely focus on the other individual and tune in to what they need to say. By not just listening to give your opinion, you can help pull yourself out of your own head and connect all the more profoundly to the moment by demonstrating appreciation to the individuals we converse with.

16. Watch your preferred show.

It is imperative to take time from your day to reward yourself, and enjoying a comfortable delight like watching a show you like can help you with stepping away from your worries and making the most of your free moments from the clamor of life.

17. Compose a haiku or any prohibitive poem.

This can move you to be innovative in manners that freestyle composing can't do, and can assist you with recovering a moment in your life that was wonderful yet brief.

18. Do a word puzzle.

GUIDED SELF-HEALING MEDITATION

Crosswords can enable your mind to be innovative and can promote your insight, as well as the general clarity of your thought. They can also give you a break from your everyday schedules, all while being fun to finish.

19. Do the dishes.

Doing the dishes can be an incredible method to take a break from life, and furthermore be profitable while you are taking a break. Washing dishes can assist you with feeling good, and it pulls you away from your present thoughts, which, thus, can give your mind consent to unwind and rest from the pressure of the day.

20. Look at an art piece you love.

Regardless of whether it is the Mona Lisa, the lyrics of a song you like, or a drawing that your spouse made, nothing is off the table here. Art is emotional, and it can help you to feel and completely immerse yourself at the moment by expressing your appreciation for the works of others.

21. Play with a pet

Feel the hide underneath your hands and the delicate quality of their skin. Petting an animal can help relieve your stress and connect you to the moment, and can pull you away from your thoughts.

At times it is easy to so busy concentrating on yourself that you neglect to appreciate the world around you. It is easy to get caught in the trap of the mundane and the range of your own objectives, and you neglect to appreciate the excellence of life and the seemingly insignificant details.

Being progressively mindful, as well as meditating, will help you remember every single good thing with time. They would help you realize that there is no sense striving hard and feeling yourself with anxiety and then ending up not enjoying your life. Meditation and mindfulness will help you get away from the struggles of everyday life and remind you to appreciate life again by taking advantage of the beauty of the present moment.

The good part of all this is that everyone has the ability to meditate and be mindful.

Meditation and mindfulness do not need to be tedious or complicated. You can, without much of a stretch, utilize any of these methods during your day to calm your mind and keep yourself focused at the moment and free from your stressors.

GUIDED SELF-HEALING MEDITATION

Simply remember to stop on occasion and take it all in.

Chapter Five: Guided Meditation to Manage Panic Attack

Panic attacks are a severe form of anxiety that makes a victim become so fearful when there is no reason to warrant such behavior. It is characterized by feelings of terror and the victim might think that they are experiencing heart failure or are about to die.

Researchers say that people usually experience a panic attack a couple of times in their lifetime, which is totally normal, considering that each one of us harbors some fears that are known only to us. But then if we develop a tendency of constantly dealing with panic attacks, say on a daily basis, then there's cause for worry.

Symptoms of panic attacks:

These are some of the symptoms felt by the victim of a panic attack:

Thunderous heartbeat

When you have been running for a long distance, you are likely to experience a higher than normal heartbeat, and even then, it's quite disturbing. But when it comes to someone who's been seized by a panic attack, they experience a wildly knocking heart that leaves them gasping for air. Their heart knocks so wildly and they feel as though they are about to die. Panic attacks are extremely uncomfortable fear response mechanisms and it's unimaginable what the sufferer goes through on a frequent basis. This wild knocking of their heart interrupts their peace, magnifies their worry and causes their productivity to take a hit.

Feeling of weakness

Panic attacks are extremely resource intensive. Once a victim has been seized by the wave of a panic attack, they normally go down and lay in a state of weakness, a clear sign of being overwhelmed. The wild beating of the heart consumes a lot of energy and makes a person feel as though they are dying. Actually, it takes some amount of time before they fully recover from the attack. It is advisable that the victim gets something nutritious to eat after a panic attack so as to discourage so that they might continue to function in a normal way.

Numbness in the fingers and toes

The wave of the panic attack is so dense that it leaves the victim feeling as though their fingers or toes have no blood. The numbness is attributed to a slight glitch in their nerves thanks to the wild knocking of their heart. But of course, they soon regain the full use of both their fingers and toes.

An impending sense of doom

As the victim of the panic attack struggles with the wildly knocking heart, they feel as though something terrible is about to happen. For instance, they might think that they are about to experience a heart attack, or as if they are about to kick the bucket. This is a testament to the intensity of the symptoms of a panic attack.

Sweating

This depends on the physiological makeup of the victim, but it is not uncommon to see beads of perspiration on a victim's face. The very thought they have been close to dying or losing the use of their heart is enough to trigger their sweat. Victims of a panic attack might still sweat at the remembrance of their symptoms.

Chest pains

Considering the wild beating of their heart during the panic attack, the victim is left nursing massive chest pains as their chest muscles align back together. It takes a while before the chest pain goes away. But the victim is likely to hold their chest all along.

Difficulty in breathing

When your heart is beating like crazy, and you are feeling as though you are about to die, and your chest is engulfed in a blanket of pain, good luck with breathing. The victim usually struggles to get air and it makes the entire scenario even grimmer. Due to their inability to breathe properly, it might bring about a small headache.

No control

In general terms, this is what victims of panic attacks feel. They cannot seem to understand what's happening. The pain in their chest, the ringing in their ears, and the numbness of their hands, all make them feel as though they have lost control. It's precisely why the victim of a panic attack hardly does anything besides act shocked.

Derealization

Some victims seem to think that whatever they are experiencing is not real. They feel as though they have been put in some other world and this must not be a reality. This goes to show that panic attacks are indeed powerful. Such victims are at the highest risk of developing chronic anxiety.

Tips for dealing with panic attacks

Once your body comes down with panic anxiety, you have the heavy task of dealing with the condition the right way.

The response that a victim gives when they face panic attacks is what determines the extent of the injury.

The following tips are designed to help you get through any form of a panic attack:

Knowledge

If you understand what our body is going through you won't be as freaked as someone who has no idea what's going on. A panic attack is a sign that your body has experienced a threat and it's in survival mode. Most of the times, these "threats" don't warrant the kind of response that the body gives. For instance, if you are a divorcee, and you happen to be strolling down the street on a fine day only to see a man that closely resembles your ex, your mind might overreact to that incident and cause you to experience a panic attack. But if you are aware of what's happening you will be less affected by the incident. Once you realize that you have this condition, it is also important to read up more on it. This will help you understand how panic attacks truly work and how you may minimize the effects and ultimately overcome this condition.

Be calm

It might seem like an easy thing but when you experience a panic attack you are bound to be anything but calm. The wild knocking of the heart, the ringing sounds inside your head, the impending sense of doom, is enough to reduce you to a nervous wreck. But then panicking about panic attacks can only make the situation worse – not better. You had better realize how to calm your nerves and develop a rigid mindset. It's the only way to emerge unscathed. Considering that the symptoms of a panic attack are quite strong, the victim must be careful to project the right attitude else it will make it hard for them to overcome this condition.

Know what triggers your panic attacks

You might not always know what is behind your panic attacks considering that your brain can magnify even the smallest of incidents. But then issues like traumatic thoughts and obsessive thoughts are potential triggers of a panic attack. You must be wary of the various lines of thinking that result in the development of panic attacks. For instance, if you were abused as a child by one of your close relatives, coming across anything that remotely reminds you of that person is enough to send you into a panic attack, but since you know that you might actually report to your brain that it's okay and dissuade yourself from developing a panic attack.

Of course, it's not as easy as it sounds but through practice, one can become perfect at understanding their emotional makeup.

In order to be able to tell what triggers your panic attacks, you must increase your self-awareness. The easiest way of increasing your self-awareness is through paying attention to your internal dialogues. Don't just waltz through incidents but take the time to understand how your mind interprets reality in relation to the emotional scars that you bear.

The worst kind of panic attack is induced by your thoughts, for then you will have a hard time hiding from your thoughts. Ensure that you have a strong sense of self-awareness so that you may be in a position to contain any potential panic attack.

For instance, if you are sitting in your office trying to be productive, and all of a sudden, automatic negative thoughts of relating to your childhood abuse crop up in your mind, instead of just entertaining these thoughts, you might want to walk into another office and share with them what's happening. In that context, your brain is less likely to feel threatened into taking action.

Mindful breathing

The thing about panic attacks is that they are involuntary. You can only act and hope that your brain won't get to that. However, if your brain decides to activate a panic attack, you are helpless. But then how you behave after experiencing a panic attack is just as important. You don't want to be the type of person that becomes crushed under worry as you remember that you were about to die.

Mindful breathing is one of the ways to calm yourself down. Mindful breathing is both a therapeutic and relaxation technique. It helps your racing mind to calm down and realize that you are no longer in danger.

Mindful breathing improves the state of your mind and allows you to savor your reality in a more intensive manner.

Conditioning your mind to experience reality as opposed to wandering off to explore your fears and worries is a great way of handling a panic attack.

Assuming that you are in an outdoor setting, then thanks to mindful breathing, you are able to savor the beauty of nature, the blueness of the sky, and you appreciate the natural world. This keeps you from entertaining the dangerous thought patterns that trigger panic attacks.

Visualization

Understand that just as your mind can lead you down the dark and horrible path of panic attacks, it can lead you into spears of light and hope.

You just have to know how to rely on your mind in order to achieve the outcome that you want. One of the best ways of relying on your mind to achieve your goal is through visualization.

There are many ultra-successful people that swear by visualization. It helps them put their fears in the backseat and focus on what they want to achieve.

Visualizing is all about calling to mind the exact thing that you want to experience in reality. For instance, if you are a basketball player, one of your important life goals might be getting the ring.

So, when you visualize, you will see yourself staging an exemplary performance and afterward taking the trophy.

Once you have visualized several times of a particular outcome, you will stop falling victim to your fears and you will develop the fortitude to fight for your dreams.

Interestingly, you can use visualization to cure yourself of panic attacks or at least reduce the effects of a panic attack.

Just get into a comfortable position and watch yourself experiencing various triggers and yet not developing any form of a panic attack.

In order to become really good at nipping in the bud negative incident and thought patterns before they blow into panic attacks, you have to have a great deal of self-awareness.

It is very easy to develop negative habits under the misconception that you are getting away from panic attacks. So, always watch out.

Be courageous

When we talk about being courageous, we don't mean that you take a spear and wander into the wild to hunt lions.

We are talking about being courageous enough to confront your reality without feeling the need to alter yourself. Not many people can accomplish that.

After experiencing a panic attack, you are likely to become too cautious about your life, and you may take on habits that will supposedly shield you against pain.

One of the habits that people commonly take is dependence on alcohol. But in as much as alcohol makes you feel better, it's only for a time, but then the bad effects come back.

You want to be the person that confronts your reality without an addiction. If you are addicted to a drug or substance, you are at risk of making decisions that will hamper your growth and development.

So, ensure that you resist various addictions that could sabotage your capacity to become a better person.

If you confront your challenges with a sober mind, there's no guarantee that you will achieve what you intended to, but there is no question you're indeed a courageous person. And it takes courage to build character.

Surround yourself with friends

Of course, there's nothing great about lying on the ground with your hands on your chest as you battle the feeling that you are about to die.

You can easily become emotionally scarred out of that experience. But if you have a great way of handling such pain then it won't affect you in a great way.

Surrounding yourself with great friends is one of the best ways of overcoming pain in your life. Friends offer us emotional support and guidance.

So, ensure that you surround yourself with friends when you suffer a panic attack.

Become aware of your physical position at the moment. It doesn't matter if you are sitting, standing or lying down. Just become aware of the place your body is.

GUIDED SELF-HEALING MEDITATION

If you want to make some changes for better comfort, you may stretch and then sit down comfortably.

(10 seconds)

Right now, you may feel as if your life is in danger and it is okay to feel this way. This is how your body and mind is responding to this moment here and now. It is neither right nor wrong.

I know that you are feeling scared because of the panic attack but it will pass.

Do you feel as if you cannot breathe properly?

(5 seconds)

You may be breathing in a good amount of air but not breathing out enough.

The good news is that we can fix it now.

Part your lips slightly and slowly push air from your system through your lips as if you are whistling. Pay attention to how the air whizzes out of your lungs completely.

Now, take a deliberate deep breath in. Can you feel how the air fills your lungs back without any effort?

(10 seconds)

Breathe out again through your mouth slowly pushing the air out.

(5 seconds)

Keep taking deep breaths.

(30 seconds)

Keep inhaling deeply and slowly push the breath out through your mouth.

(30 seconds)

Now, allow your body to adapt to its natural rhythm of breathing.

(30 seconds)

In case you feel like your breathing is becoming strained again, become more deliberate about ensuring that you are exhaling completely.

(30 seconds)

You are safe and in no danger at all. Panic attacks are horrible and may make you feel physically uncomfortable but that is all there is.

You are in no danger.

(10 seconds)

GUIDED SELF-HEALING MEDITATION

Now bring your attention to your body. Feel as your shoulders drop to their natural position and the muscles around them become relaxed.

(10 seconds)

Are you clenching your jaw? Loosen your jaw abit and allow it to relax. Let your tongue rest between your lower set of teeth. Parts your lips slightly so that they are not too tightly closed against each other.

(10 seconds)

Notice how your heartrate. It is beginning to slow down. Soon, it will resume its normal rate.

(10 seconds)

Notice your breathing is becoming deeper, calmer and quieter.

(10 seconds)

Allow yourself to relax.

(10 seconds)

Listen to the following affirmations. They will help your thoughts to calm down.

I know that I am safe.

(3 seconds)

I have the ability to overcome panic attacks.

(3 seconds)

I am aware that these panic attacks cannot harm me.

(3 seconds)

I am okay and safe even though my heart is racing.

(3 seconds)

I am calm.

(3 seconds)

I can envision what relaxation feels like.

(3 seconds)

I can envision my whole body feeling centered and relaxed.

(3 seconds)

I am safe and calm.

(3 seconds)

I know that I am safe.

(3 seconds)

I have the ability to overcome panic attacks.

GUIDED SELF-HEALING MEDITATION

(3 seconds)

I am aware that these panic attacks cannot harm me.

(3 seconds)

I am okay and safe even though my heart is racing.

(3 seconds)

I am calm.

(3 seconds)

I can envision what relaxation feels like.

(3 seconds)

I can envision my whole body feeling centered and relaxed.

(3 seconds)

I am safe and calm.

(10 seconds)

Now, begin to count backwards from 100, 99,98,96….

(30 seconds)

In this moment, here and now, you are safe. Allow yourself to get calm.

(30 seconds)

Now pay attention to your breathing. Do not adjust your breathing but notice as you breathe in and as you exhale.

(10 seconds)

Start to count each complete breath. A complete breath is made up of one inhale and a subsequent exhale.

(20 seconds)

Keep counting your breaths and when you lose count, simply start from the beginning.

(30 seconds)

Continue to notice and count each breath.

(90 seconds)

You are now calm and relaxed.

(5 seconds)

You are now calm and relaxed.

(5 seconds)

You are now calm and relaxed.

(5 seconds)

GUIDED SELF-HEALING MEDITATION

Let your body and mind continue to relax and calm down.

(60 seconds)

When you feel ready, you can open your eyes and familiarize with your surroundings.

Chapter six: Deep Sleep techniques

Meditation to Overcome Insomnia

Whether you find it difficult to sleep at night as a result of stress, tiredness, work or several other factors, or you find your sleep unsatisfactory, you might be suffering from insomnia. Insomnia is commonly called difficulty falling asleep, or staying awake, and there two types of insomnia.

Acute insomnia is mostly caused as a result of lifestyle, or circumstances. A security officer on night duty will find it difficult to fall asleep on duty, likewise a first-time dad may find it difficult to fall asleep thinking of his precious wife in labor.

While, chronic insomnia is a complicated type of insomnia. There is no known underlying cause, yet the individual finds it difficult to either fall asleep, or sleep at night for long hours. Such person may also experience disrupted sleep, for more than 3 times a week.

Experiencing insomnia regularly causes mood disturbances, fatigue, stress and difficulty concentrating. Although, insomnia can be caused by factors like anxiety, work related stress, lifestyle, and sicknesses. However, the approach to overcome insomnia is not easy for some persons, yet there is one possible way to overcome not just insomnia but enjoy a long, satisfactory sleep for the rest of your life.

How Does Meditation Cure Insomnia

Meditation is a relaxation technique worth trying, which can help improve your sleep, make you fall asleep easily and also make your sleep satisfactory, such that you wake up feeling refreshed. Meditation harmonizes the mind and body, and also influences the brain and the way it functions. The effect of meditation on your mind and body is that you become calm, and relaxed afterwards.

Effect of Meditation on Insomnia

During meditation, the mind is focused on one thing, which prevents the mind from wandering. Your mind and thoughts are brought to the now moment during meditation. Hence, anxiety disappears and it becomes easier to fall asleep.

During the meditation, your mind and body are been connected to each other, and they both become relaxed and calm, which helps you sleep as soon as you get in bed.

Furthermore, meditation helps boost the hormone called melatonin that regulates the sleep and wake cycle. Without stress, the melatonin level is usually at its peak at night to ensure you get a sound, and restful sleep. However, the presence of stress among other factors that causes insomnia, the melatonin level drastically reduces, thereby insomnia occurs. With meditation, the melatonin level increases because stress has been reduced, and the body is in a relaxed state.

Meditation Techniques for Insomnia

If you want to experience an undisrupted sleep, an intense meditation must be done frequently. There are different techniques of meditating for insomnia and understanding process help us to get started immediately.

• Cognitive shuffling

Cognitive shuffling is a simple meditation technique that can be done alone. It is simply a do-it-yourself technique that shuffles your thoughts to sleep. Here is how cognitive shuffling works, when you lie on your bed, your mind is likely to be filled with different thoughts from your daily activities. You can be worried, and anxious about your bills, relationship, the next day activities, such that you find it difficult to fall asleep. The effect of this shuffling on the brain is it tricks the mind to get into a dreaming state.

Tips to Practice Cognitive Shuffling

- Firstly, getting in bed is important

GUIDED SELF-HEALING MEDITATION

- Right there on your bed, avoid focusing your concerns. Let your deadline be, the bills, the complicated issue at work. Let it all be.

- Now that your mind is free from your fears and worries, create a new engagement like imagining objects, places, names or movies to meditate on. You can imagine different things, like a teddy bear, a fish, a dog, the sky, the rainbow, or the ocean. Note that, the items you are imagining should not be threatening or scary. For instance, instead of imagining an ocean because you have the fear of water, you can imagine the rainbow or the sky with beautiful stars.

- Ensure your eyes are closed before you begin the cognitive shuffling process.

- Process should be repeated if you are still awake, until you run out of words.

SA Ta Na Ma (Mantra)

Sa Ta Na Ma is a powerful meditation technique that works on the brain and its functions to reduce risk of depression and other mental illness. It is a mantra that is usually recited in 3 voices; the singing voice which stands for the action voice.

The whispered voice which stands for your inner voice, and

The silent voice is known as your spirit's voice.

SA TA NA MA chant describes the evolutionary aspect of the universe. Each word in the chant has a meaning.

SA means the beginning.

TA means existence and creativeness

NA means death or the end of life

MA means rebirth

The effect of this mantra is displayed by a balance in emotions, and a settled mind.

Practical steps to Sa Ta Na Ma

- Find a comfortable position. You can sit down or lie down.

- Decide on how many minutes you want to recite the mantra.

- Breathe in and out through your nose and mouth and ensure you sigh after this breathing exercise is heard.

- Close your eyes properly, and place your hands either on your lap, or knee. Make sure your palm is facing up.

-Begin chanting slowly, and press the thumb of your hands, with your four fingers. Count your fingers each starting from the thumb to recite the mantra.

GUIDED SELF-HEALING MEDITATION

- Keep reciting the chant as a calm and slow pace

During recitation, you have to follow the principles of the mantra.

When you mention SA, you count from your index to your thumb

You count from your middle finger to your thumb when you sing TA

You count from your ring finder to thumb when you recite NA

And final you should count from your pinky finger to the thumb when you mention MA.

- Still in that position, sing SA TA NA MA in a loud voice, your voice should be audible, and ensure you move each of your fingers with each sound. The more you sing, the more you feel relaxed and energetic. However, your soul and spirit should feel relaxed and enjoy the sensation which is moving through your body and mind.

- When you feel relaxed, shift your focus and start singing in a whisper voice. At this point, energy is flowing through the body, waist, and knee.

- Next, be focused on silence. Continue counting your fingers and silently repeat the mantra to yourself.

- After singing the mantra completely, breathe in and breathe out with your arms wide open, and lift the hand above your head. Release your hands down, and exhale again. Repeat process until you feel refreshed or drowsy.

What to Expect When Meditating To Fall Asleep

Your expectations when meditating to fall asleep is most likely to have a sound and deep sleep at night, except you are uncertain about the benefits of meditation. Meditation for sleep is similar to other kind of meditation; however, the approach to each of these meditations is what matters.

When meditating, your meditation technique determines what you will have to do. Albeit, you can start preparing for your meditation exercise, by breathing in and out, lying flat on your back. If you are having a guided meditation, all you need to do is follow the instructions instead of been worried about what to do and what not to do.

Furthermore, all you should when meditating to fall asleep is sleep, but try to avoid any form of distractions.

How to Meditate Before Sleep

There are two ways you can meditate before going to bed, it can be a mindful meditation where you pay more attention to your body and mind, and also having a guided meditation where someone leads you through the process of meditation.

Mindfulness meditation can be done alone, in your own room house and house. While guided meditation is a very easy meditation, it is just for you to follow and listen to instructions from a guide.

Guided Meditation Tips for insomnia

Guided meditation is the form of meditation you engage in with the help of a tutor, or instructor. Ensure that you will not be disturbed, during the course of this meditation.

- Lay down on your back, preferably on your bed or mat. Make sure you are comfortable on whatever you are lying on.

- Close your eyes and prepare your mind for the meditation you are about to engage in.

-Breathe in and out, ensure that your breathing out is audible such that it looks like you breathing out heavily. Make your body feel the heaviness, after which your body will be relaxed.

- Pay more attention to your breathing, and you feel easiness. A natural breathing process.

- At this point, you will feel your body is relaxed. Feel the way your breath travels through your lungs, and hold your breath. As this is happening, you will begin to feel relaxation in your body.

- You can begin to breathe normally right now, and as you breathe you feel your muscles, joints, and back relaxed.

- Pay more attention to your stomach area right now, where your abdominal muscles are present. Tighten the muscles in your abdomen, and hold your breath for 10 seconds and release your muscles. During this release, feel the difference the tightness of your abdominal muscle and the relaxation of these muscles.

- Repeat the above process 5 times.

- Breathe in and out, tighten your abdomen and release it to relaxation.

Feet

-Divert your attention to your feet, and make them relaxed. The relaxation should be from your toes to your ankles. Tighten your toes and feet, and feel them become heavy and relaxed.

-Focus on your nails, feel them relaxed and let go.

GUIDED SELF-HEALING MEDITATION

-Pay attention to your thigh area, and feel them relaxed.

- Again, focus on your waist, lower and upper back, joints and feel them relaxed. You will feel the feel heavy, and very relaxed

Upper limbs

-At this point, focus your attention on your arms. Feel them heavy and relaxed.

- Get a sense of how heavy your arm is, and feel the relaxation shift to your elbow, wrist, and fingers become very relaxed.

Face, neck and facial muscles

- Shift your focus to your facial muscles, neck and face.

-Every muscle in your face, your cheeks and chin becomes relaxed, and your entire body is now relaxed.

A deeper meditation for the abdomen

- Locate your center, which is your abdominal region. Imagine there is a bowl on your abdomen. Slowly see the bowl rolling over your abdomen area, and it relaxes every muscle the bowl rolls in contact with.

-The bowl now moves slowly from your abdomen area to your right hip carefully and softly massaging the muscles of the hips it comes in contact to.

-Massaging back and forth all the muscles in your abdomen.

-The ball continues to roll over to your knee, and around your knee. You can feel the tension on your navel melting away. Roll the ball slowly to your toe, and over to your toes, from your small toes to the big toes.

Every part of your body this ball comes in contact with feel the part of your body relaxing.

-Now feel the ball begins to roll upwards away from your toes again. Massaging and reducing tension around your toes, knees, ankles and rolls over to your center, your abdominal area.

-Again, this balls rolls to your left thigh, and your knee, massaging both the back and front of your knee.

With your ball you move this ball to wherever you choose, and how long you want it to be.

-With this ball, massage your knee, and ankle and toes. This ball touches every muscle in your toes, it gently massages them and at this point, you feel your muscle relax.

GUIDED SELF-HEALING MEDITATION

- Feel the ball roll back up your leg, your knee and thigh muscle and arriving back at your center.

-Shift the focus of the ball to the base of your spinal cord. Allow the ball rest there for 5 seconds, and allow it move up your spine, and near your heart. At this point, you can feel the ball massaging the internal organs in your body. The ball massages the heart, and you feel relaxed.

- The ball rolls to your throat area, and the back of your neck area. You feel your neck area relaxing after the ball massages it. You feel tension reducing around your neck area.

-The ball travels down your arm, and to your wrist. The ball gently massages your wrist, and fingers.

-You feel the ball roll up your arm, to your shoulder and neck. It travels down to your elbow, forearm, and wrist and into the palm of your hands.

- Allow the ball gently massage your palm, and fingers. The ball moves up your arm, shoulder and face and as it reaches up in your face, the ball splits into a hundred tiny balls. You feel them travel around your face, to your eyes, eyebrow, cheeks, chin, teeth, tongue and teeth.

- You feel the ball massaging your face and every part of your face. At this point, you should enjoy this facial massage.

- Imagine as you are lying down the ceiling of your house. Your eyes are still closed, so imagine the ceiling of your room opening itself up, and the roof also opens itself open.

-Still looking at this opening, you will see the beautiful white sky. The sky is clear, bright, and the moon is out and also full, filled with stars. This is a magical peaceful night. You are alone, safe in the beautiful part of your house.

-Watch the twinkling and beautiful little stars, looking down on you and you are enjoying the peace of the night.

- You look again at the stars again, the little ones that are thousands of miles away are not shining so beautiful like the big star closer to you, which is looking at you directly from the sky.

-You are looking deep into galaxy, beyond time, you see a million other stars waiting for you and shining at you.

- Take a deep breath. Breathe in a rich air from the infinite and beautiful galaxy filled with stars.

- Feel yourself been a part of these stars, there is no separation between you and them. Feel you are already a part of this wonderful galaxy.

-As you experience this, you become a shooting star, shining across the galaxy like others.

-Slowly you begin to fade into the sky, into the unending space and galaxy.

-You are living in the wonders of this space, where there is neither time, past or future. You feel you are the stars, the moon, and you occupy the pace between the planets.

-You are floating off slowly, as you travel across this universe; you feel your body wants to drift away. You feel peace, wholeness, and love.

-When you are ready, and feel relaxed, you can let go of the galaxy. When you drift off, you will drift into a peaceful and wonderful sleep.

Guided Meditation for Insomnia in Pregnant Women

Meditation for pregnant women can seem difficult; however, the need to be relaxed is very important, to reduce tension, and frustration. Below are some tips to help you meditate as a pregnant woman.

-Pick a comfortable position, you can lie on your back, or sit upright. Ensure you feel comfortable.

- Take a deep breath, and take another deep breath for your baby.

-You are aware of your strong, beautiful and shaped body. You are aware of your baby and how beautiful the baby is.

-Ensure that you feel and observe the sensation that comes as you breathe in and out. As you are breathing in, your body is getting relaxed, and tension is reduced.

- Remember that you are pregnant and meditation can be difficult as this stage; however, take your time to be patient while meditating. Try to avoid every form of distraction around you.

- Find a quiet place to be alone for 10 – 15 minutes. Sit in an upright position, and make sure you are comfortable.

- If you are lying in bed, focus your attention on the bed, by imagining that you are sinking into bed. And if you are sitting, create an imagination of your body in contact with your mattress, and also sinking into it.

-Begin to sense what it feels like to sink into your bed. Notice if you feel lighter, or heavy. Then begin

GUIDED SELF-HEALING MEDITATION

awareness on your body to observe any tension and tightness around your body, from your head to toe.

- Focus your attention on any part of your body you desire, and become aware of the part of the body. Breathe in and out. Get a picture of that part, feel the tension melting away and tightness reducing.

- You can scan your body part 2times in 5 minutes. During this scan, observe and note places that are relaxed or still tight.

-Practice more breathing pattern here. Breathe in and breathe out, for the first 2 minutes, observe your breathing pattern, and focus on your breathing, without a motive to change it. You may start to notice that your breathing becomes slower on its own. You may also notice the way your body moves when you breathe. If your chest rises more than your belly does, it means your breathing is shallow.

-However, a shallow breathing is just a pattern that shows our state of relaxation. If you are relaxed, your belly will rise more than your chest.

-Place your hands on your bell, and feel your baby.

- Observe the movements in your belly with your hands,

- Think about your day, in a structured way. Look back at every activity you did during the day.

Remember when your baby kicked, when you went to see the doctor, when you had a funny and interesting conversation with your friends. Be patient to watch these moments as your brain play them back for you. These flashbacks may seem long or short, it all depends on how your day went. Keep enjoying this flashback, focus your mind on it and avoid been distracted and watch as these events unfold to the present moment.

- Shift your focus back to your baby. Place your attention on your feet, toes and tell them to switch off. You can literally say the word 'switch off' out so that you feel you have told your body parts they are not needed until the next day.

- Repeat exercise and inform your upper limbs, your arms, hands, wrist and fingers to switch off.

- Repeat your breathing exercise again.

- Place your hands on your belly, and say the following words

You are a miracle, and not a trouble.

You will allow me have a restful night

You will be patient with me till I am awake.

You are healthy and strong."

GUIDED SELF-HEALING MEDITATION

-After saying those words, breathe in and out gain for yourself and your baby.

-Imagine that your baby is falling asleep. Pay more attention on how your baby looks and the way your baby breathes.

- At this point, I believe you should be asleep. If you are not yet asleep, you can repeat exercise and allow your mind get relaxed.

Guided meditation for Insomnia in children

Guided meditation is a type of meditation, where there is an instructor. Little children do not have to that the knowledge to meditate on their own, so their parents can guide them into this meditation using the following.

-Welcome to your happy moment. We will start an adventure right now.

-Make sure you are lying down properly, on your bed, if you feel pain because of the way you lie down, let your parent or guardian know.

- Close your eyes properly and begin to imagine things the sun, how it is so clear and shining. Do not open your eyes.

-Start releasing your body, and everything you are thinking of. So, tighten your muscles, your arms and legs, for a few seconds.

- Let your arms get released, with your legs too. Enjoy the relaxation now, as your muscles are released

-Try the process again, tighten your arms and legs and release them later.

- Start breathing in and breathing out. Make sure you hear the sound that comes out when you breathe in and out.

- Release the air you have breathed in from your lungs, and breathe out.

- Repeat the breathing exercise, breathe in and out and relaxed.

-Now, imagine yourself in a beautiful and dark garden like the wonderland. This wonderland is dark, because it is night.

-You feel the ground is so soft that you feel like sinking into it.

- You feel a gentle and soft breeze on your face and body. The wonderland is so cool and beautiful; you don't want to leave there.

- At this point, you see your body becoming relaxed.

GUIDED SELF-HEALING MEDITATION

- You look up, and set the beautiful sun set, and the birds flying around in the wonderland.

-You continue walking; you look at the beautiful trees, with fruits on it.

-You keep walking until you see a colorful tent in front of you. The tent is the color of the rainbow. It is so beautiful; you walk into the tent.

-As you go into the tent, you see how beautiful it is. It has a beautiful sofa with the rainbow color, the wall of the tent has the pictures of all your heroes, and you like the way the tent is.

-The tents has different rooms, the living room has a Television set with your favorite cartoon, the kitchen has the pictures of your favorite food, the room has big soft bed, you feel the softness as you touch it, and there is a big pool where you can swim before the kitchen.

- Keep walking around to see how beautiful this tent is.

- Now, you are done looking around this magical tent in your wonderland. You walk out of the tent, and you see another beautiful garden that surrounds the tent.

-This garden is so beautiful. You are walking around and you see a table with two chairs, a jug of juice, and two glass cups.

- You drink a glass of juice, and look around to see if there is anyone around you.

- You then see someone walking towards you; the person is smiling at you. The person is happy, and keeps smiling at you.

- You offer the person a glass of juice, the person receives it happily and drinks.

-You show this person around your magical tent.

- Did you have a beautiful talk with your new friend?

- You hug your visitor softly, and you watch the person go away.

- You breathe in and out and you feel happy and relaxed right now.

- At this point you are feeling sleepy, so you walk back into the tent and walk into your room to lie on your soft and rainbow color bed.

- You tuck yourself into your bed, and place your head on the soft pillow.

- You feel your body sinking into your bed. Your arms are feeling relaxed, and your hips to your toes are feeling relaxed.

GUIDED SELF-HEALING MEDITATION

- There is a window in your room, so you lie on your side to watch the beautiful dark sky and you also see the big shining star in the center of the sky.

- You smile and feel happy; you tell yourself you are a big shining star.

- You look at the other shining stars; they look beautiful just for you.

- You see them moving together fast; you wonder where they are going. They are going to the galaxy, so you decide to join them.

- You see yourself floating into the dark clouds, and far beyond the clouds, you see more stars.

- You are happy now, and very sleepy.

- You begin to drift away. You are getting sleepier, so you return to your soft bed.

- You cannot open our eyes now, because you are already deep into your sleep.

- You mind and body is now relaxed and quiet.

- At this point, you are fast asleep.

Conclusion

The mind is the engine of the body, it is what carrying that bulk of muscle, that heavy brain on your head; it is what keep you going. You exercise the body to keep it fit and ensure it functions at par and as expected, you eat good food and take drugs to handle and conditions the body when it faces some issues that you are familiar with; you read to get the brain fired up, to help the brain do its work and functions properly. But when it comes to the mind, that engine room, one thing that ensures it stays fit, that helps it combat any unfamiliar issues it is facing is meditation.

Just as you are being diligent to out nutrition and brains enhancements through reading, you also have to be diligent to your medications. No matter how busy you are, no matter how tight your schedule is, just as you cannot miss your breakfast, just as you make it a habit to read the morning paper and a book, it is important that you put in same diligence and consistency into meditation to enhance your mind, to keep it stable.

Meditation keeps the mind strong and defends it against external attacks. Draft it in to your schedule and your calendar, because a stable mind, a well-conditioned mind is the anchor you need.

The next step is to stop reading and to get started practicing mindfulness meditation, or the others meditations (choose what you feel more suitable for you), as frequently as possible. While initially, you may not feel as though you are getting very much out of the time that you put in, the more you keep at it, the more quickly the positive benefits of being mindful are going to start stacking up. Don't get discouraged if at first, you find that your mind remains unruly; every moment you spend fully engrossed at the moment will make it easier to reach the desired mental state in the future. Take it one step at a time, and you will soon find yourself fully engaged in the present without even trying.

To your success!

© Spiritual Awakening Accademy

www.ingramcontent.com/pod-product-compliance
Lightning Source LLC
Chambersburg PA
CBHW050251120526
44590CB00016B/2299